1
OUT-OF
CHURCH
CHRISTIANS

BY ANDREW STROM

Why are tens of thousands of devoted Christians leaving the churches? Is it a 'movement'? What is causing this world-wide phenomenon?

RevivalSchool

THE OUT-OF-CHURCH CHRISTIANS

NOTE: Due to space considerations a number of the emails quoted in this book have been abridged. Otherwise the book would be much longer than it is! Often we had space to publish only one or two paragraphs from each – or even just a few comments. At times it has also been necessary to correct grammar or punctuation errors, or make similar minor alterations. For legal reasons and privacy considerations there have also been a few occasions when names or places needed to be removed. In every case, we believe the original thrust and intent of the author has been retained.

Published by: Revival School
www.revivalschool.com

Wholesale distribution by Lightning Source, Inc.

Scripture taken from the New King James Version®. Copyright © 1982 by Thomas Nelson, Inc. Used by permission. All rights reserved. [Sometimes the KJV is also quoted].

ISBN-13: 978-0-9799073-5-7   ISBN-10: 0-9799073-5-7

1. Christian Life: Pop Culture Issues   2. Revival

CONTENTS:

CHAPTER ONE

A WORLD-WIDE PHENOMENON

For me, this whole "snowball effect" began with a Radio show and an email. In March 2003 I was invited onto the Rhema Christian network in New Zealand to discuss the growing phenomenon of "Out-of-church Christians". I had been invited onto the show because in one of my books I had recounted my own 'wilderness' experience and the fact that many Christians seem to be opting out of today's church system. This was a phenomenon that I knew something about, but even then I had little idea of the size or scope of what was occurring.

The same week that I was on the Radio show, I published an article on the same topic on our international Email List. The result was an absolute deluge of responses from all over the world. Below is the email I sent out. I had no idea that it would set-off such a chain-reaction.

EMAIL: RE: "OUT OF CHURCH" CHRISTIANS
Andrew Strom. [4 April 2003].

I am writing on a rather unusual topic today. On Monday night (31 March) I was invited onto a Christian Radio show in New Zealand to discuss the growing numbers of "Out-of-church" Christians in the West – people who have left the churches for various reasons but still claim a strong Christian faith. It was a very interesting night, and the phones ran hot.

This "Out-of-church" phenomenon has now grown so large that books are being written about it. In fact, several years ago I heard an estimate that there are TENS OF THOUSANDS of such Christians just in our largest city (Auckland) alone. And I believe it is the same right across the Western nations. I have personally come into contact with literally hundreds of such people. The surprising thing is that they are often the most committed kind of Christians – praying, insightful, deep-thinking. Yet they have grown tired of "playing the game" inside our church system and have opted out. Often their involvement goes back many years. In fact, they had commonly been leaders of various kinds.

But now they have left. Why? The church obviously finds this a very difficult thing to explain or deal with. The usual accusations are often trotted out: "So-and-so has been hurt and has a root of bitterness". Or they are in "rebellion". Or they are "not a team player". Or they are "backsliding".

But if you talk to these people you will often find that they have been sitting in church for years and years, and they simply cannot stand to sit and watch the same old game being played any more. The LACK OF GOD is what gets to them – even in our most "Spirit-filled" churches. WHERE IS GOD IN ALL OF OUR ACTIVITY? Surely this is not the way it is supposed to be? New fads and programs come and go, but the mediocrity and LACK OF GOD just seem to go on forever. And so quietly, sometimes without anyone even noticing, they slowly slip out the doors – never to return. Some have even told me that they felt God "calling them out". Others simply felt they couldn't stay there anymore. The state of the church weighed upon them more than words could say.

Very often they did the rounds of other churches, hoping against hope that they would find a place that felt "right" in any way (though most of them are not "church-hoppers" by nature). But the places they visited never seemed any more "right" than the place they had left. And after a while it just seemed easier to stay at home with God.

As I said earlier, most of these people have not given up on Christianity at all. It is today's church system that they have given up on. And we are talking about large numbers here.

Thousands are already opting out. And many feel like they are "waiting" for something.

Some of these people have started up home-fellowships. Or they meet with other couples on a casual basis. But many meet with nobody at all, and they consider themselves in a 'Wilderness' place – alone with God. (Very common).

I was asked several weeks ago by a pastor whether I agreed that what is happening could be a 'move of God'. That is a pretty radical thought. Many leaders would think the opposite. Because anything that leads people out of "their church" can't be of God, can it?

Hmmmm. All I know is this: The concept of going through a 'Wilderness' just before entering the 'Promised Land' is totally Scriptural. In fact, it is right through the Bible. Even Jesus went through such a wilderness time.

But it is not possible to stay "alone" forever. Someday, if these people are going to be part of a new move of God's Spirit, they are going to have to come out of their wilderness and become part of the "BODY" that Jesus brings together – the 'new wineskin' that will come with this new move of God. Otherwise they could miss out. That is the great danger.

I'm sure there are many on this List with comments or testimonies relating to this topic. I would love to hear from you. It really is becoming a significant issue in the church.
God bless you, my friends.

For weeks after I published the above article, I was inundated with emails. It seemed to be going round and round on the internet because many responses were from people that were not even part of our own List. Such a huge number of heart-felt stories from people who still loved Jesus but had left the churches (forever, in many cases). What an eye-opener! It confirmed to me that this issue is so much larger than many of us have realized. I don't think a lot of Christian leaders have any clue how many believers are simply opting out of "organized religion" today.

Throughout this book you will read many of these stories, sent to me from all over the world. To give you an understanding of just how "global" this phenomenon is, here is a small sampling just to get you started:

From: Ian (Scotland):

We are a group of 4 Christians who meet in our respective homes. We were formerly leaders in our local fellowship, but for various reasons found ourselves outside of the established church. And like yourselves we have found the we are not alone. We have met with dozens of Christians around Scotland who are in the same boat. Most were leaders in their fellowships. We were with a group last night of two families with about 8 or 9 meeting in a home.

Your estimate about the number of people in this position does feel about right. I have been in contact with one man in London who has a mailing list of four thousand. I have heard that estimates would put the total as being greater than those that are still in 'Church'. But due to the nature of being 'out of church', it will be very difficult to quantify.

From: Pastor Jim C. (USA):

In my estimation, in regard to the numbers involved per capita, New Zealand has the sniffles and America has full blown pneumonia.

From: Mary (USA)

You would be VERY surprised at the number of VERY high-level, gifted and mature Christian leaders who are NOT attending regular church here in Southern California. My husband and I hosted a care group about 7 years ago with 15 couples. Only 3 of them still attend church.

From: Thomas (USA):

My family and I are, I believe, some of the millions who have left the church system or have been called out by God into the "wilderness." As the Lord explained our calling out He said it would be a time of purging and teaching us to stand in Him alone so that we could stand properly when we are brought back with the many. We still fellowship and share the Word with others. We still, at His direction, do the works of the Church: meeting the needs of others and sharing His truth. We are just not part of the system and I don't believe we will ever be called to rejoin a religious system, but a living fruit-producing Body.

From: Mike (Vineyard Church, UK):

Just read your piece on 'Out of Church Christians'. Amazing – I've been getting an increasing sense that this is what is going on around us here in the UK. So many fine Christians living effectively outside the Body... and I've always felt that anyone who amputated themselves like this would die and rot, like a severed finger – yet these guys don't, or haven't yet, anyway. The loss to the church is one thing, and the danger to them another – and yet there is this wilderness thing. Look at King David, how he had to spend all those years running in the desert before his anointing could take effect, as it were...

From: Donnalea (South Africa):

This phenomenon has reached our country too. I'm sure that many out-of-church South African Christians have already contacted you. Although I am still in fellowship, I have really been going through a tough time getting myself to church every Sunday. I love the Lord with all my heart, but Christians and modern day Christianity or "churchianity" get on my nerves. I too am tired of all the programmes and never once seeing or feeling that God is in control. I desperately want to know God again and to really know His will. I am in fellowship during the week with people who have left church completely and as with this general phenomenon, are true Christians really seeking God's will.

From: Tony (South Africa):

I read your article on "Out of church Christians" with much interest, and yes, it is a worldwide phenomenon. I have personally spoken to many Christians from abroad, many of them business men (it seems like the business community was almost the first to identify it). And yes, what started off as a trickle, well, now the flood gates are open and many have either left, or are in the process of leaving.

From: Jouko (Finland):

You just described my situation in your article "Out of church" Christians. There are many in that position in Finland, too. I don't know what will be the future solution for this dilemma.

From: Liz (Zimbabwe):

Have just received your article from a friend and was most interested to discover that it is not only our country which is experiencing this "phenomenon" (if I may use that expression!). There are many of us who have felt "called out of the church" and group together for home cells where there are about 12 folks together. Then once a month we meet up with others, but have a very strong prayer network and are in contact daily with each other, as needs are great here in Zimbabwe.

From: Mark (USA):

I am still in church leadership and music ministry in a traditional church setting, but many very anointed & prophetically gifted friends of mine have had their fill of "playing church" and have "opted out" of organized religion. One is running a ministry (camp/retreat) for pastors in CO, another is raising sheep in KS, a third is creating an online network for churches, but none go to the traditional 'sermon/music/prayer/pulpit & pew' places we call "churches". I feel in my heart that this mass of hungry and Christ following people is God's own way of setting the stage for a huge reformational change.

From: Randy (USA):

I read an explanation of why the phenomenon is growing – the out-of-church Christians. They say that we are lone rangers, backsliders, not team players, have bitter root judgments.... This can't be further from the truth.

When we have been attending church, we find – No God – No Power – No Gospel – Bad Agendas – Poor Leadership – Bad teaching – Bad programs – No Christ – No Healing – No miracles. Just a struggle for personal power and control.

I can't tell you how many times I have been treated like I am not going to Heaven because I am not attending church. So, the sad part is, where do we take our gifts, our tithes, and our love – but out to the streets.

We know many who have left the church, who are committed as prayer warriors, intercessors, missionaries, and worshippers. Wanting to share their gifts from God.

This movement is growing – so it will over-take the church. What you are seeing is just the tip of the iceberg.

From: Pat (Canada):

I've been an out of church believer for over 7 years. I'm also a non-denominational ordained minister. I've visited a variety of churches over the years (and spoken at many of them) as the

Lord led, but to be honest I frequently find it very hard to visit them. It's as if all I can hear are sobbing people and the rattling of chains all around me, yet everyone is smiling and singing of how God has freed them and filled them with joy. Often I feel like crying while believers around me are smiling and laughing with apparent joy... yet in reality they seem to touch very few with the love of God... even in their own churches. Canada has as many, if not more true believers who are also un-churched as New Zealand has.

From: Sam (ex-Vineyard pastor, Canada):

I live in a community of 330,000 people and the OUT OF CHURCH Christian population has grown from 6,000 to over 10,000 since the summer of 1999...

From: Sue (Australia):

I personally know a lot of strong Christian committed ex-church leaders, sold out for God, who God is using outside the local church. Some are in home groups, some just get together regularly for fellowship. As for me, most of my fellowship is with my friends in NZ and Australia by telephone and email.

From: Jenny (New Zealand):

I work alongside people who have left churches as my job, under the umbrella name of Spirited Exchanges. I facilitate a couple of groups for people to process what has gone on for them in churches and to struggle with the faith and church issues...

I would agree with you – the accusations of 'backslider' and others are quite inaccurate and unhelpful. From what I have seen they are actually asking the hard questions in order to deepen, continue in and better integrate their faith.

I too, wonder if there is a move of God in this – people being called to something deeper, out of the game-playing and conformist faith stage...

From: Scott (Japan-based email):

As a person who has been involved with ministry and with churches heavily for over 20 years (right from when I was 15), I can understand why people just leave. In the old days, we would give messages about that kind of person and say that they were lacking in commitment, and how you have to be planted in the one place, and how everything God wants to do he does through the local church, etc.

So people who dropped out of church were always seen as having not much to offer.

But, there are tons of them out there. I have chatted recently and am surprised that a lot of people who do want fellowship, and love God, don't go to a church regularly.

From: Anne (USA):

In America, in certain cities, the out of church Christians are probably higher in number than the in-church Christians. It is a phenomenal occurrence... I feel as a missionary evangelist that there are so many church programs with little or none of the Presence of the Lord in the churches and that is the reason people leave them. There is little prayer and what prayer there is is void of passion and power and fire.

From: Peggy (USA):

My husband and I have been Christians for 30 years, home group leaders for much of that time; my husband has also been a worship leader for most of that time. However, now we are among the "out of church" that your message describes, although we do continue to meet and pray with other believers who feel the same longing for something more real than we *have experienced for longer than we care to remember. The cry of our hearts is *not* to live on our memories of incredible intimacy with God in years past, but to discover Him anew and in deeper ways than ever before. We are desperate for Him. In light of that hunger, the emptiness of our church experience, a church we'd attended for 17 years, was more than we could bear.*

The above are just a smattering of the hundreds of emails I received on this subject from all over the world. Several days after I published the original article a Webmaster from France wrote saying he had translated it into French and put it on a French website. After that I started getting all kinds of emails in French – none of which I could read! Which just goes to show that this "Out-of-church" thing is a huge issue right across the Western world. Everywhere, it seems, people are hungering and thirsting for the REALITY of God, but sadly no longer finding it in our churches. What on earth is going on?

CHAPTER TWO

MY OWN "WILDERNESS" EXPERIENCE

One of the reasons I was originally invited onto that Radio show was because in theory I was someone who could see "both sides" of this issue. I am a Christian speaker who holds meetings and speaks in churches, but I am also someone who has spent seven years completely "out of church" – in the wilderness, up until 1993. And to this day I have many friends and acquaintances who are out there still. So I understand this phenomenon well.

My own 'wilderness' experience has been a very important part of my life-story. It had an enormous impact on me. I have never been ashamed of this experience, and it has long been available for people to read about on my web-sites and in one of my books. The following version is virtually lifted straight off one of our web-pages. Hopefully by reading it you will come to understand some of the 'phases' I went through during my wilderness journey. It has certainly stirred up a lot of comment over the years.

"MY WILDERNESS EXPERIENCE"
By Andrew Strom

I had been brought up in a Christian environment all my life. My father was a Spirit-filled Baptist preacher before I was born, and was also a researcher and writer on Revival (it runs in the family!). So when I myself became a Spirit-filled Christian at the age of 17, I was fascinated with Revival and prayer right from the beginning. I also came under a very powerful 'prophetic' anointing, though I had little understanding of it at the time. (What was "wrong" with me? Why was I so distressed and devastated at the condition of the church when others seemed so comfortable with the status quo?). Fortunately I had all my Revival books which told me I was not alone, but merely one of many concerned Christians, right down through the ages. But I certainly felt very much alone a great deal of the time. (Apart from God of course – He was always there).

I became involved in a couple of churches – the main one being a fairly "hard-line" Pentecostal group. And because of my very brash youthful zeal in witnessing I did alright there, though I seemed to be always in some kind of trouble with the leadership. I just couldn't shut my mouth at the crucial time – I so longed to see the church in a true Revival state, and I was pretty brazen about my opinions (I certainly lacked for wisdom in those days!). I was also very "hard-line" legalistic myself in many ways. But God was training me and using me, almost in spite of myself.

But then it happened. Finally, after many run-ins and minor disputes, I came across what I felt were some pretty fundamental differences in doctrine between this church and me, and I finally left for good, after chafing for quite some time. But instead of going looking for another church, my wife and I banded together with some friends and tried to start our own group. But whereas before God's blessing had been with us, now it clearly was not, and nothing much came of what we were doing. God had some BIG lessons in store.

This was the beginning of a period of literally SEVEN YEARS totally outside the church system (from age twenty to twenty-seven) for myself and my family. (By this time I was married to a wonderful Christian wife and we were to have six lovely children).

All through this period of wilderness, testing and spiritual trials, one thing I never gave up on was my nightly prayer-times with God. These were as blessed as ever, but often they were the only 'spiritual' thing I had going on in my life. Everything else seemed closed, empty, dead. This went on for year after year after year. I KNEW we were not to go back to church, yet nothing was happening. But if I visited a church, nothing was there for us either. All was desolation, and in the end I (who had once been the proudest, loudest, most hard-line arrogant witnessing machine) was so spiritually "crushed" that I could hardly bear to talk about spiritual things with anyone. Some may say that all of this was of the devil. Not so. GOD had led me out into the wilderness for a purpose, and He would lead me in from it in His good time. I was being humbled and broken, and every ounce of proud 'religious' life was being crushed out of me, that God might one day shine through.

During this time we slowly became aware of a network of "out-of-church" Christians right through New Zealand (and no doubt in many other countries also), who had all come out of various churches (some had even been leaders). We would occasionally visit them on a casual basis, and we found that there were almost out-of-church "doctrines" amongst this group, which we came to imbibe ourselves. Much of this "doctrine" was more negative than positive. It often involved long litanies of everything that was wrong with the church system and its leaders (a very soft and convenient target), often involving somewhat "mocking" sarcasm, and relief that we, the 'real' Christians were now out of it all. I fully partook in all of this with great relish, having my own chip on my shoulder, and my own resentments to nurse. And of course, the great "answer" that we smugly believed in, was to leave the churches altogether. We became quite suspicious of 'churchy' Christians who were still in the system – even if they were praying people who obviously walked close to God. How arrogant we were, once again! But after awhile even this began to pall, and I became so 'crushed' eventually that even mockery of the 'system' gave me little joy any more. All was vanity, all was nothingness. When would God ever move?

We got involved with Christian music (my wife and I are both musicians), but we were just banging our head against a brick wall during this whole period. God had us in 'prison', and we were going NOWHERE until we learned what He had to teach us. I had been praying for years, "God use me, God fill me more

- 17 -

and more with your Spirit, God bring Revival", and here I was sitting in a spiritual 'dungeon' – and there was nothing I could do about it. Spiritually speaking, it was like being in a kind of "crushing machine". I was almost in despair at times. But this is what you will get if you ask God to 'break you and use you'. Don't be surprised if He takes you at your word!

My first band had become almost an "idol" to me by this stage (I was 26 years old) – as ministries often do. But one day, something dramatic went wrong that meant we would have to cancel a concert, and suddenly I KNEW – I just KNEW that this whole thing was not of God – it was me striving, striving, striving to "MAKE IT HAPPEN". And I knew in that instant that it was all over. This was my last holdout – the only spiritual ministry I had left, and it was not of God. The band was finished. We played our last couple of concerts and that was it. THERE WAS NOTHING ELSE. NOTHING BUT GOD.

And instead of striving and 'ministry-idolatry', I began to once again spend hours just basking in the presence of God, tears streaming down my face, just glorying in His presence – worshipping and communing with Him. And I began to come under a prophetic anointing the like of which I had never known, even at the beginning. I was 27 years old, and I had been in the Wilderness for seven years.

Suddenly God seemed to remove the old cloak of heaviness and replace it with a garment of praise. And He kept telling me the same thing over and over again: "REVIVAL IS COMING. REVIVAL IS COMING." (Sometimes I would literally leap for joy at the reality of this word). During one intense three-day period, God showed me how I could attack and destroy in Jesus' name, many of the strongholds of pride, rebellion, religion, etc, that had had a hold in my life for many years. And this is literally what I did. Glory to God! I tell you, I was transformed. And God also began to introduce me to many praying and prophetic people (mostly 'in-church', though some were "out" – I didn't care what format or 'boxes' they fellowshipped in any more – their relationship with God was what mattered). Many of these people confirmed what God had been showing me about the coming Revival. And I also heard my first 'prophetic' tapes from overseas, which were amazing confirmation. Suddenly I was not alone! All those things God had been showing me down the years – He was showing others too! Suddenly, I began to feel I needed to write it all down, so others could share in what God was saying. (I hadn't been writing for years). No longer was I crushed and despairing in the Wilderness. I was mightily free in Jesus. But something important in me (in fact, a lot of things) had changed through this Wilderness journey. I was not the same person in many ways. (In fact many people could not believe the changes). God had crushed me and brought me to life again – His way. And many of the "rough edges" were gone forever. I was now far more reliant on Him – for everything. These were very crucial changes, and indeed, I think now, how could God ever have used me the way I was??

I am now 39 years old. My wife and I have been happily married now for nineteen years, and we have six wonderful children. We eventually became quite involved in a local Spirit-filled Salvation Army church, then a Baptist fellowship, before relocating to America in 2004. I myself have been in full-time ministry now for a number of years. But I am convinced, like many of you, that the best (and the most challenging) is yet to come, and that glorious Revival lies just around the corner.

There are two points arising from all this that I would like to make. The first is that I believe God took me out of the church system mostly because of the faults in ME – more than in the church. (Though it is obvious that today's church does have serious problems, of course). He wanted to get me away into a desolate place and get rid of my arrogance, my pride, my brashness, my "hard-line" legalistic view of things. He also later dealt with my "superior", smug attitude towards 'churchy' Christians and systems, etc. He wanted to break me and humble me (at my request) because only then could He truly use me.

What a devastating process! But how skilfully managed by God. He desires not to destroy us, but to save us from ourselves. How dark our hearts are, and how much we need to be broken and re-made in the image of His holy Son.

I believe that many prophetic people (like myself in those days) do have problems with "rebellion". They seem to rub leaders the wrong way almost by design sometimes. And then they develop a "persecution complex" or slink off wallowing in self-pity. I have done all of this and more. Rebellion is the most insidious sin, and when you begin to see how much it dominates our world, and how ingrained it is in us, it is a real eye-opener. This has been an absolute revelation to me in recent years. How deceitfully wicked is the heart of man!

On the other hand, I empathize with prophets speaking an unpopular word that comes from God's own heart, and being rejected. What a devastating experience for a prophet. I have been in these situations also. But I have found that it is only when you have dealt with Rebellion that you can truly trust yourself to speak God's word to a leader. Rebellion can greatly affect the words we bring to leaders, and yet many prophets seem to hardly know they have a problem in this area. I can look back now and I wince at the influence of Rebellion over my words and actions in the past. But God does cleanse and heal.

The other thing about Prophetic people and "out-of-church" types is the 'individualism' that can easily set in, and make them of little use to God in any real way, because they just cannot truly relate to a 'Body'. It is simply not possible to have a Body made up of individualists. It just does not work. A true Body has LEADERS. It has members who are "KNITTED TOGETHER". I am often amazed when I come across 'out-of-church' type material which encourages rampant individualism (i.e., coming out of church and "doing your own thing in God") and then goes on to talk about the wonderful Revival that is coming. I tell you, unless you can KNIT INTO THE BODY and relate well to leaders, and all the other 'Body' things, YOU WILL NEVER

HAVE A PART IN THE COMING REVIVAL. It is just a pipe-dream. Some say they will relate well to the coming leaders, though they have trouble with all of today's leaders. Let me tell you: God is dealing with Rebellion now. If you can't sit under authority today, you will be a pain in the neck to tomorrow's leaders too. Deal with your rebellion now, or miss out. It's that simple.

My second point is that the Wilderness IS a valid place to be for people who are being broken, trained and molded by God. Many of God's heroes, big and small, down the ages, have been personally dealt with by God in the Wilderness. And I believe that many of those whom God has been preparing to have a part in His new move have been taken through the Wilderness by God in our day. The Wilderness is not the answer in itself. It is a waypoint. If you get stuck in the Wilderness, like the children of Israel did, you are in trouble. If you like the look of the Wilderness more than the Promised Land, you are in BIG trouble. The Wilderness swallowed most of the children of Israel whole. They did not use it as preparation, like they were supposed to. They went to the place of testing and failed the test. But historically, the Wilderness has been a very important place of brokenness and training, where God has prepared men and women before using them in some way.

So I ask those who are "in church" not to belittle what is happening in the lives of some whom God has 'called out' for a time, just as I would ask that they not belittle you. There is much truth in the concept of God using the Wilderness not so much to get people "out of the system", but rather to "get the system out of people". We have got to un-learn many of our old 'Christendom' habits for this coming Revival, so as not to repeat them. The coming Revival cannot be caught up in conventional "churchianity" as we know it. For this would ruin it, as it has ruined many Revivals down the ages. Thus, 'un-learning' is one very important reason why I believe God has taken so many people out of Christendom for awhile, into the Wilderness. It is preparation for the coming Revival, which will be very different from now (but also very practical – just like the early church).

My hope in writing this has been to challenge both groups – those within and those without the system, to prepare in whatever way God would have you, for what He is about to do. And to promote understanding of the different paths that He has been leading His people on.

CHAPTER THREE

WHY ARE THEY LEAVING?

"It is nevertheless my contention that the number of leavers from evangelical, Pentecostal and charismatic churches is much larger than previously anticipated and that the rate of leave-taking is increasing." -Pastor Alan Jamieson, author of 'A Churchless Faith'.

There have been a number of publications that have referred to this "Out-of-church" phenomenon in recent years. Charisma magazine did a major write-up in a February 2005 cover-story entitled, 'When Christians Quit Church'. They noted that "an alarming number of Christians are staying home on Sunday mornings" and quoted Christian pollster George Barna's research that 13 million "BORN AGAIN" believers in America no longer attend church on Sunday. The Barna Group itself released a piece in 2005 entitled, 'TREND: Significant increase in out-of-church Christianity.' In it they noted that the number of un-churched adults in America is growing at the staggering rate of ONE MILLION per year. (Source: www.barna.org). In addition to all of this, the author of the World Christian Encyclopedia, David Barrett, estimates that there are around 112 million "churchless Christians" worldwide – about 5 percent of all adherents. He projects that this number will double by 2025.

New Zealand pastor Alan Jamieson, author of 'A Churchless Faith', has been studying this phenomenon for some years. To his surprise he found that far from being nominal churchgoers, 94% of the 'out-of-church' Christians he interviewed had previously been leaders of some kind – such as deacons, elders or Sunday school teachers – and 40% had been full-time Christian workers. He also found that for many the break came not because they had lost their faith, but more because they wanted to save it.

Sadly, Jamieson says that many churches seem unaware – and unconcerned – about those who have departed their ranks. The vast majority of leavers that he interviewed told him that no-one from their church had ever discussed with them why they had left.

I myself have discovered that there are a wide variety of reasons for people leaving, and a wide variety of situations that they find themselves in today. Some have joined the ranks of the new house-church networks that are rising up all over the world. Many more, however, are opting for a more spontaneous or non-structured form of Christianity. Some have even left regular Christian fellowship altogether. For them this truly is a 'wilderness' experience – alone with God. I am sure you will recognize these various experiences in the emails below.

What I want to do in this book, is spend a number of chapters looking at the reasons why these people are leaving. After that, I want to look at the validity of what they are doing, and finally what it would take for them to become involved with the wider Body again.

Even though some of the things that these people say about the church could be classed as "negative", I believe it is absolutely vital that we hear from them at this time. Because what they are saying is representative of thousands of people who are deserting our churches in their droves right now. And we need to take urgent notice of their reasons for doing so. We might not like what they are saying, but we really do need to listen – for our own benefit as well as theirs.

Let's start by hearing from several leaders who have left behind the normal format of "church" to become involved with 'house-church' – an extremely fast-growing trend around the world right now:

From: Ron (New Zealand):

I have been a pastor for several years and have seen and experienced many of the deficiencies in today's church. I saw many people who lived in mediocrity, trying to fit God into their lives instead of trying to fit their lives into God. While there are many good people in church and good churches, I too had been left feeling there had to be more.

What God started to reveal to me was that there is not one way to have church. Since becoming a Christian 17 years ago I have only known the "community church" way of having church. What I have subsequently come to learn is something Larry Kreider, International director of Dove Ministries explains well – there are emerging different models of church.

The traditional model has been the "community church" where the pastor leads the church, the church runs various programmes and meets in a community building. This is like your local 4-square or New World supermarket.

Also emerging in the last 20 years is the "mega-church model". This has co-incided with the introduction of WalMart in the USA, The Warehouse in New Zealand, where people travel for miles to go to a big, impressive "one stop" shop.

However, more interestingly is the emergence of micro-church networks. These are small group churches, house churches or similar, networking together for support, vision and accountability. These networks have sprung up all over the world, mostly under the direction of the Holy Spirit (not an imported model!). The small groups are more intimate, relational, real, and made up of people who live counter-culturally. Outreach is relational and very effective. These groups rather than growing larger keep multiplying and planting more churches that become part of the network.

This is a phenomenon that has really only come to prominence in the last 3-5 years. It appeals particularly to generation X and Y'ers because of its strong relational element.

From: Sam (Canada):

I was on staff in a Vineyard church, and I resigned in 1999 after an intimate encounter with the Lord through reading the word of God and Tommy Tenney's GOD CHASERS. I resigned a week after my last sermon. I could not play the game anymore.

I discovered that my mechanic, an elder at a local Pentecostal church and a friend of 17 years had opted out as well, and he was meeting with Christians in homes and their commitment to the Lord did not diminish. In fact it grew!

I discovered another group of people who had walked away from the system. They had essentially become a community. Some still lived in their homes, but some had sold theirs and then pooled their resources and bought a larger house so they could all live together. And they have been together since 1968. I discovered other believers who would gather at Tim Hortons, our version of Starbucks, a coffee shop, and would talk and pray and encourage each other. I discovered too that in some of our larger malls, Christians were gathering there on Sunday mornings to walk with other people and exercise and then have a time of fellowship and share needs and what the Lord was doing in their lives.

All these and more testified to opting out of the system and a desire for authentic Christianity. They and myself have given up on the religious system that is presumed to be authentic, but we see the church as the people of God, and not the trappings of ministry, buildings, tithes and offerings, and program after program. We want nothing to do with that stuff.

I started hanging out with others who were just as disappointed as I was. We just got together, and we ate and hung out and we fellowshipped. We brought our kids, and we played games and celebrated life. We worshipped and shared the word, we helped each other out, and cared for some obvious needs in each other's lives and did some mercy ministry and outreach in the city. After a year of this, in November of 2000, I asked everybody (18 of us) that we should seek the Lord about becoming an organized church. We fasted and prayed for a month. We then gathered and talked about what we thought the Lord was saying. Oddly enough, it was this: "Keep doing what you are doing, for this is why I have called you out and gathered you together. You already are the church and you are becoming more and more the people I desire you to be."

This staggered me. I was ready to plant a cell church, and here, the Lord was already telling us that we were the church He wanted us to be! Needless to say, we have pressed on and continued in this journey. We have become obsessed with the Lord and intimate with Him and we have developed much stronger relationships with the Lord and each other, and we understand more fully all the "one another" passages in the NT, and especially the "love one another" passages. I am amazed at what has happened. I would never go back to what I knew before. Never.

I am now networking with others, and have found that there are over a dozen such house churches in my twin cities, and there are more springing up all the time. I have discovered fellow Vineyard pastors have now transitioned three of their churches to house church networks. There are networks who are discovering new ways of expressing the life of Jesus and His ministries in a variety of wineskins... we believe that this is a definite new paradigm of church life being unleashed in North America.

From: Kristine (USA):

So how did "house church" happen for me? Well, a couple of years ago my small "prophetic group" that was meeting under a larger church stayed together and became a house church. And then much to our delight, we found out about 15 more house churches during a "house church gathering" that was at a home. Many of us have interconnected and go to each other's house church for various teachings, intercession nights, or just "get together, eat and enjoy each other night". Our house church has also connected with a house church that feeds the homeless every Sunday at a local park (which was very difficult for me to get used to since we were actually doing what Jesus said to do, "Feed the poor"). And now we do Sunday "church" in a park. It's not about "US" anymore.... it's about "THEM!"

From: Zack & Patty (USA):

As for us, we could not play church any more. The church we belonged to was supposed to be a five-fold-ministry church where people were to be equipped so they could do what God was calling them to do. As it turned out, it became a works church with programs, liturgy and control. Our former Pastor micro-managed all aspects of the church. From worship to retreats.

My husband was the worship leader. The micro-managing got so bad that he was told how to do worship. God and the leading of the Holy Spirit were totally removed from the picture. He finally couldn't handle it any longer. He had to choose God!! He had to quit... and do what God was calling him to do... worship Him in freedom! As for me, I was a church leader in women's ministry and a deaconess.

Since we have quit the church we have been called rebellious, dead wood, and we have been accused of having the spirit of Jezebel. Sad, isn't it... All we wanted was Jesus and for Him to be lifted up!

After we quit the church we had people who wanted to worship and enjoy God's presence through the gift God has given my husband. So God has developed a home worship and praise group which I have nick-named The Acts II Gang. Each time we meet, someone gets healed or is ministered to by God and the power of His Holy Spirit. We currently have had 10 to 15 people attending.

This is what God has called my husband to do... Lead Worship to the place where people come to a greater understanding of God's love and to experience God's marvelous touch. So sad to think that if this had been allowed, this same kind of ministry could have happened in our former church.

We want to be part of God's movement... We want to lift up His church... not man's agenda church... We want to see Jesus lifted up and people coming to know Him in a real way...

Quite aside from those who are departing from conventional churches to hold meetings in their homes, there are large numbers of Christians who are simply opting out altogether. For some it is because of one particularly bad experience in church – or sometimes a whole series of bad experiences:

From: Bob (USA):

The church across the street, a Church of Christ, is holding revival meetings through the weekend. Our front porch sets up high overlooking the street. Kay and I sat watching as they gathered. Some might look up, few, if any will speak, though we have tried.

It's been a while for us, so long since "going to church". This evening, as we sat out there remembering those days, it may have been, say, at least fifteen years from the last one, beginning from the mid 70's in a Nazarene Church. We wondered about those we knew back then, wondering how they might be today, successful remembering some names, associating others with certain events, memories fading or lost. We were involved heavily in their activities, though never "card carrying" members. They brought us in and truly loved us, I believe. Both Kay and I agreed that we missed those friendships with three or four couples who took to us, visiting in each others' homes, events planned to include many numbers of church folks. It all seemed good to me, these social relationships.

Our second summer, they appointed me to represent the softball team in the local church league. It was my job to manage the team. I settled my expectations, thinking it would be a cake walk. After all, I was dealing with mostly all Christian men, in it for the exercise and fellowship.... no fierce competitors to face, no nasty attitudes or dispositions. I had seen it all before, participating in city leagues, in army leagues, that win-at-all-cost pressure cooker that sometimes creates hard feelings, and in the extreme, even physical confrontations. Never in a church league!

Phil was a tag-along, always eager to help, to do something. If we were designated as "home-team", it was also my job to see that the field was prepared for playing. Grass cut, base lines chalked, ready to go. None to help me, yet Phil was always there. Back then, he would have been about 19, and somewhat "slow", both physically and mentally challenged, yet, only slightly. Though in the eyes of a few, he might have been "in the way", I knew Phil just wanted a friend and to be one.... and I also knew he wanted to play softball. Boy, my illusions would start to crumble, big time. Phil was no ball player, but what the hey.... it was a church league, folks with big hearts and charitable natures. I would let him play.

Right field would be the place for him. It would be rare that Phil would have to catch anything. Knowing that this particular team had no lefties... I watched as one smart aleck stepped to the plate on the wrong side. His intentions were obvious, knowing Phil's ability to catch anything was about 1 chance in 100 or so. I would kinda hold my breath. It wouldn't help.... Phil missed a routine fly ball, and just a couple of the guys were really mad at me. "Get him out of there!"

"Awww.... come on guys, it's just for fun, it's just a game, let's let him play." One in particular got in my face, threw a bat to *the ground.... "I'm here to win, if you're not, then I'm wasting my time".... and off he went, got in his car and drove home. I stood there in shock, hurt, puzzled, confused.... Only Phil came to me. "It's ok Bob, I don't want you to get in trouble, I'll sit down." It broke my heart, it truly did.*

Now, I will tell you, this thing happened so many years ago, yet so fresh still because of it's impact, I cannot forget. The "best" is yet to tell. So much at a loss as to what to do and how to handle it, I sought out the "associate pastor", who was there at the game to witness the spectacle..... "Bob, don't worry. If he should quit coming to church, it will be no great loss. He doesn't tithe that much anyway." In an instant, many of my images came tumbling down. How clearly I understood the value of a man. A new building was going up, and my thoughts went back to the previous Sunday morning as the pastor's sermon was on tithing. "I've been looking over the books back there, and some of you are either not making anything or you are robbing God." Now here was the other "preacher" making it very clear..... money.

We watched them this evening going to church.... obvious their kinship, their friendship, their conversation. We sat in silence for a time..... then Kay sadly said, "I miss that." I know her heart, and what she really meant...... and I said, "I do too, babe, I do too."

From: Terrie (USA):

Several years ago, I also left my own church, weeping uncontrollably because of the grief in my spirit. While the minister stood to preach, women (mostly) wandered up and down the aisles, and across the front, jerking and making chicken-like movements. The ministers evidently thought it was God. I have never spoken against them, or against anything they were engaged in, as I am just a sheep. But I did not and will not participate. Since then, church splits have taken place and it appears that the leadership has gained at least some discernment. It appears to me that well-meaning, but undiscerning and ignorant sheep are drawn into these things. The Holy Spirit can do some really strange things. I've seen and done some myself while under His influence. But some of this was not God.

Others who have left say they just could not stomach the predictability of the same old "routine" any more. Where was the life? Where was the vitality of Christ? To them, even many of the so-called 'Spirit-filled' churches seemed to be quite dull and predictable. It became harder and harder to force themselves to go along each week:

From: Shawn Marie (Cayman Islands):

I also am a believer that has been hiding out at home intimately with the Lord, because of so much emptiness, boredom, and frustration in the churches, and I'm talking about Holy Spirit-Filled Churches. I am in the Cayman Islands and I fellowship with believers around the world on the internet. So many are hurting and left hurting by the wayside for lack of spiritual food – "starvation"! I do believe that we are on the brink of a whole new spiritual outbursting and explosion and rising up of a whole new strong army of the Lord.

From: Chris & Rick (USA):

We're NOT "rebellious" or "mavericks" or baby Christians.... We've been saved 20+ years, have a grown son who LOVES Jesus and is a Worship Pastor, were previous "church leaders", and have had a Prison Ministry for 7 years.... We just cannot seem to be able to stomach the "routine" of weekly going to hear the same guy come up with ANOTHER message....

From: Bill & Bonnie (Canada):

We have been so frustrated with the church for several years. The word is no longer preached, and what is said is the "Spirit of God moving" many times certainly is not. I have prayed and asked the Lord to show us where we can find other believers who are hungry for Jesus too. We have been accused of backsliding and church hopping. We have gone to several churches but have not been able to find one where Jesus is exalted.

Quite a number of those who wrote had seen too many double-standards in the church – preaching one thing and doing another. After awhile it had affected their very desire to be there. They did not want to leave but over time it all got too much:

From: Geralyn (USA):

I am one of those Christians that is having a hard time finding a church that is acting like the church, in the book of Acts – in the Bible. I am so tired of many Christian Churches being controlled by one person (Pastor, Priest, Rev., etc). God's idea of the church (ecclesia) is not what is going on in most churches. He wanted all to be equal in importance and using different spiritual gifts to make the Church prosper. He had elders in the church, He had teachers, disciples and apostles. We need to get out of the mindset of going to church and to realize we are to BE the church. We should be a body of believers with specific jobs to bring the gospel to a lost world. Teaching in churches is important. But, there comes a time when we have to do what we are taught. Live what we are taught to do. So many Christians are looking too much like this world and not like children of God. We need to live a life different than everyone else, so non-Christians become hungry for what we have.

From: Douglas (USA):

It's better to be real with the Lord than go to church and play the holier-than-thou church game everyone seems to play there.... until you meet them out of church in their everyday life and you see how those holier-than-thou's are really living... That is where God wants us... in our real lives not the pretend ones most people feel they must behave like at church... He loves us how we really are.

From: D.D. (USA):

We were church leaders, pillars of the faith, and prayer warriors and intercessors with 20-30 years of faithfully working within the church... But men seem to be cursed by some kind of turf-war mentality and more concerned with their own empire building of personal ministry than with building the kingdom of God... We came to the sad conclusion after many years that the 'powers that be' at the top of church structure didn't really want a 'church' built after the pattern that God laid out in the Bible at all... but rather something built after the pattern of the business world... Think about it: What if Noah hadn't built the Ark according to the pattern God gave him?... What if Solomon hadn't built the temple according to the pattern God gave David?... Until the 'church' that Jesus died to birth is built according to His pattern, you're going to see more and more sickened and leave a church that is all program-oriented with no 'true' move of God.

From: Mary Jean (USA):

We have seen it all. From dead, compromising churches to hyped-up phoney churches, telling us that if we just do this or that, the next level will come. And of course, the biggest doctrine of our generation, if you just give more money, all your problems will be solved, or worse, He will heal you, fix your marriage, flood you with lots of money, etc.

From: Michelle (USA):

I wandered away from the Lord for many years, and just recently found my way back to Him. Or more accurately, He said "Enough!" and I obeyed. I've tried to go back. The last time

I went, the pastor was preaching and he had such a spirit of disillusionment that I could hardly stand it. It's as if he couldn't make himself believe it anymore. That's my feeling in general. Church is social time. Time to dress-up and participate in "holy" gossip. The gifts are denied, there's no concern for the true needs of the brethren, and sin is candy-coated...

From: Vicki (USA):

I left my home church (charismatic, multicultural, North American) eight months ago. I have visited other churches and begged the Holy Spirit to give me guidance as to what to do. I miss the fellowship, the security, and the guidance that a congregation can give to the individual.

Recently, I visited my old congregation. I thought perhaps I was to return and nothing but my silly pride was keeping me from doing what G-d wanted me to do. I am tired of being alone and without a spiritual family for emotional support. But I came away with the same old impressions. Leadership wants my tithes, my presence and unquestioning obedience. And most of the Christians want a 'warm and light-hearted' Christianity...

From: Marlene (New Zealand):

I am one of those 'wilderness' Christians you talk about in your email. For me, I am totally convinced that what I am feeling and experiencing is 'of God'. The way it all started for me was: I was asked to join the leadership of a new church a couple of years ago now. I found that I was deeply burdened for the state of the churches at that time. Often in the middle of worship I would be overcome with a spirit of intercession and would weep almost uncontrollably. The feeling was of great sorrow and grief. When asking the Lord for some understanding, the only thing I got was that his presence was grieved. I felt that he had left the church and that we were doing business as usual without really acknowledging him. I believe the church corporately has lost its way. God is saying enough is enough. I have moved recently to another city, and there is more life in one of the churches I have attended, but I think overall the games and familiarity have become so ingrained in many lives that many people wouldn't know if God was there or not. I am loathe to support something that is not functioning effectively. Where is his presence in our corporate gatherings? It's time to cry out to God and say, I will not give up until you come! Many people I talk to feel exactly the same. I am a deeply committed Christian of some 20 years. I did not leave church because of bitterness or hurt. -Simply because it is not doing the works of God!

Others had a lot to say about the way church is set-up today, and the fact that it does not seem to be particularly biblical or Christ-like in their view. These people often had some very interesting things to say:

From: Orlando (USA):

Clearly this "system" of Church that has been developed, recognized and accepted among many who are a part of what is considered "mainline Christianity" is not functioning according to the New Testament Church example that is given in the Scriptures. Instead of an actively living, growing, reproducing, unified and boundless organism (the Body of Christ), what has been formed is just an incorporated organization, private social club for the elite...

The very evidence that supports the fact that today's church system is not set up according to the New Testament Church standard are such phrases as "church hoppers", "my church/ your church" or even the question "who's church are you a member of?" These very phrases have become a very common and accepted part of the vast majority of Christians' vocabulary.

From: Richard (USA):

My friend, Church is not, and I say again NOT, some place that you go. Church is something that you ARE. If you are not the Church, then going to some building in a pretext is not going to make you Church. You can put a horse in the garage, but that doesn't make him a car.

From: Marcia (New Zealand):

In the Christian world it is very much like the secular world – i.e., "What do you do?" Occupation determines who you are. With Christians – "What church do you attend?" determines who you are in Christ. So wrong – but it happens regularly. I hope one day people will stop doing this. I have not been attached to a church for 2 years now. I am very comfortable with my God who is really the delight of my soul. He understands me like no other.

From: Betty (USA):

I found Jesus as my Savior when I was six years old, in a Foursquare church. I am now 57. I spent most of those years in the church system. And I was involved in the "ministry" of the church. I taught Sunday School, led the choir, played the piano, was two Pastor's secretary. But my heart always longed for more. So I found Aglow, Full Gospel Business Men's, home meetings. Always searching. About 10 years ago I remember asking Jesus, "Jesus, is this the church You said You would build?" By this time I was heart sick with the church and all its man's programs and lack of the presence and moving of God. About the same time someone gave me a book that opened my eyes and heart to see the truth of the five-fold in Eph 4. And I could see how that would never fit into the current church governmental structure.

I went from church to church for quite awhile, always hoping that I would find one with the truth. But no. It is such a hard place to be, a wilderness. I long for corporate worship. I worship the Lord alone at home but without a doubt there is a dynamic to corporate worship that I am missing. You are right, we cannot stay out here in the wilderness, eventually we must come together. But.... we cannot bring about this "coming together" of Jesus's Church. Only He can.

Some of the emails I received were from people who had found it extremely liberating to be free of all the activities and restrictions of "church as we know it". They were now able to achieve far more for God than they ever had before. One delightful email came from a group of four elderly women who are now getting an astonishing amount done:

From: Pat (USA):

Our little group has been free to do all sorts of ministry that we probably would never have done or even known about had we been busy with church activities. We've done 3 Alpha courses (2 of the young people who came to the Lord in our first Alpha are now ministering in drama at a huge church), we organized and participate in a group that works with the incarcerated young people in the local bootcamp. We've worked with the local youth. Three of us serve on the board of a ministry which is an outreach to the community... We support, both financially and spiritually, a local missionary to Mozambique. We sponsored a women's retreat... I teach a Bible class weekly at a local assisted living facility while another of our group is the CWA regional chairperson. One has become a licensed drug counselor and is doing Christian drug counseling. Another has a retreat center as her business.

We are doing what we could not do if we were in a traditional church. If four older women can have this much ministry, just think what could happen if people stopped looking at the back of each other's heads and started taking the great commission seriously... Here are, a small group of women but empowered by a mighty God! What would happen if all who are anointed for ministry were free to move as the Spirit leads?

It is important to remember that the emails published in this book are representative of many thousands of Christians who are opting out of our churches in record numbers right now. I myself received hundreds and hundreds of replies to my original article – but it is only possible to publish a fraction of them here. This movement is huge. It is happening on a global scale and anecdotal evidence suggests that it is growing at a phenomenal rate. For every email published in this book, there were many others sent to me expressing similar concerns. We have to face the facts: Thousands of devoted, praying Christians are leaving our churches – many never to return. As we have heard, pollster George Barna has collected data that shows there are 13 million of them in America alone. And we desperately need to listen to their reasons as to why they are leaving.

CHAPTER FOUR

"CALLED OUT"?

A significant portion of the people who wrote to me were adamant that the major reason they had left the churches was because they felt "called out" by God. It was not because they were "hurt" or offended or any other reason. They insisted that they had received a call from God to "come aside" and so that is what they did. In this chapter we will take a look at what these particular Christians said about their reasons for leaving:

From: Anne (New Zealand):

I do not come from a background of hurt. I have been out of the structure of the Church for 3.5 years after I very clearly heard the Lord call me out. I am not sure I am going through a wilderness experience as such, but more of a time of growth in learning and total dependence upon my very faithful, closest friend. I am open to going back into the 'system', but not until God calls me in, as clearly as He called me out.

From: Sue (Australia):

I too sensed that God was "calling me out" – and even though I had the usual Scripture verses quoted at me, and had it insinuated that I too was being "rebellious", "not willing to be under authority" etc, etc. But the sense of God's calling was so strong that I just had to heed it.

I didn't leave my church without telling my pastors why I was doing so. This was a church that was so "seeker-friendly" that what it was serving up was even less than spiritual milk. I informed my pastors that I needed spiritual meat. They seemed quite happy with the idea of one of their flock leaving because she needed meat; I'm sure they are continuing on with their "You can have a happy life" series of meetings, with a few references to God thrown in here and there.

Funnily enough, I have grown stronger in the Lord and learnt more in the two years I have been out of the church than the eight years I was in it...

From: Pete (New Zealand):

I felt 'called out' a year ago and went through a very difficult and trying time both within myself and from the Christian community. I have spent long hours in prayer and in seeking God for answers to something that quite frankly broke my heart. While the persecution continues somewhat I have come to know God and my Lord Jesus Christ in a much deeper and more personal way than I ever thought possible within 'the church'.

I realize now that God wanted me to come to rely on Him and Him alone for my growth and sustenance and while I was well into leadership roles within the denominational system it was not where God wanted me. We have started our own home fellowship called "Reaching Out" Christian fellowship and we have now a number of others attending regular Sunday fellowship and Friday night prayer groups. We are ministering in the community to those who are less fortunate and to folk who just need help and we are reaching people that the churches seem to be unable to reach. We feel strongly that this is just the beginning and that God is building a foundation among His people.

From: Darcy (USA):

Since the Lord "called me out" of the church that my family was a member of, I/we have suffered great condemnation, misunderstanding and criticism for our decision to follow the Lord rather than man. It has been difficult and there have been many times when I just wanted to walk away from "fellow believers" who keep asking me, "Where are you going to church now?" When I tell them that I am not going to any church at this time, they are quick to either invite me to their church (I have tried them all) or they judge me and tell me that I am forsaking the assembling of ourselves together. For a long period of time I was in a state of being numb from it all. Then, the Lord kept bringing people into my life who were in the same boat. What a gift it was to know that I was not alone.

There were also many Out-of-church people who spoke of a far greater 'intimacy' with Jesus now that they had left all the activity and bustle of church life behind. The Bible tells us that the greatest commandment is to "Love the Lord your God with all your heart, and all your mind, and all your soul, and all your strength." Such an overwhelming love for God can only be developed through "seeking Him with all our heart". I have noticed that there is a very strong emphasis on this kind of close personal relationship with Jesus amongst many Out-of-church people. It really is a dominant theme of many of the emails I received, as you will see below:

From: Robin (USA):

I am no longer hungry for Jesus, I am Starving for Him and He isn't in my local churches! I obeyed His calling to just rest in Him and I have been doing this for almost 4 years now. When the Lord calls me back in, I will run for I know what His voice sounds like for my ear has been pressed upon His chest for a long time now. I am not full of rebellion against the churches for I cry out for their eyes to be open so that they too will learn to go deeper into Papa, an intimacy that nothing in this world could ever fulfill!
We are the church, not the four walls that have been built! These walls must come down and embrace the lost with His love, embrace one another with His hunger, His Fire, and we will never be the same again! I do believe the time is coming very soon when all who have been called out and have been resting and waiting upon the Lord will be called back in, but

with them will be His torch that will set the hearts on fire!

From: Louise (Australia):

I have been out of mainline "church" for 2 years now and the Lord has led me on a much deeper and intimate journey in that time. I have found new fresh freedom in our relationship and consequently find the "church" systems only that... systems which are ultimately man made and man centred. It has been a time where I have learned to go directly to the throne for all wisdom and He has been faithful. The Scripture, "Draw near to the throne of God and He will draw near to you" has been a daily drink.

From: Cindi (USA):

I have seen this for quite some time as like a mass EXODUS of God's disciples who truly hunger and thirst for God's REAL life and intimacy and a REAL daily walk with our Father... Did you know Webster's defines religion as "back to bondage"? The majority of so-called denominations of every NAME have been so involved in their own "agendas" for so long they have either forgotten or have never known total dependency on Christ and His Holy Spirit... And many of us who have left have discovered God personally in a way that is indescribably powerful and intimate and radically different from the ways we were taught through church services.

From: David (Canada):

I have been an "elder" and involved in more than one denomination. Eventually I came to the place where I had to stop everything. It was a very real encounter and the result was a "Woe is me" much like Isaiah as I caught a glimpse of what my sinful nature is really like and how so very much of all that I had ever done was for me in His Name. A hired hand, not a friend. I had prayed for revival, for His Presence in the church, you name it. The answer was to begin to see Him and abhor myself. I could not go on. Not one step. No-one understood what had happened to me, least of all me.

The fellowship that I enjoy is freer and deeper and more marvellous than it has ever been. None of it occurs within traditional boundaries. None. He has led us into the desert to speak tenderly to us. It's a place where there is only wilderness and Him. No distractions. He then makes the wilderness into a fruitful garden.

From: Lorraine (Location unknown):

I am one of the 'some' who you mentioned as having heard the Lord call them to 'come out' of the system and get alone with Him. From experiencing this one on one with Him for the past 3 ½ years I can honestly tell you that nothing can compare to how wonderful it is to grow closer and closer to Him in intimacy every day. My relationship with the Lord has deepened in every way through this experience. It is impossible to describe how real He has become in my life. Everything I do and say revolves around what He is telling me to do or say. In this place of aloneness with Him, He has proven Himself to be enough!

Many think in their minds that 'aloneness' with Him, means outside of the Body. They think that this means that those outside the system do not fellowship with other believers. I don't know about others, but I have more fellowship with other believers now than I did when I was still in the system. The fellowship with others that flows from this intimacy with the Lord is so much more honest, open, and fulfilling than the fellowship that I had with others when I was in the system. It is real, heartfelt, communing with other believers. It is completely a Spirit to Spirit connection, rather than a natural gesture of being friendly towards others because they go to the same church as you. I feel more a part of the Body now than I ever did when I was sitting in a natural building full of people.

The one thing the system can't offer to believers is intimate relationship with their God. The system can offer us numerous fleshly activities, but has no power to affect the inward heart of mankind. Outside the system I have encountered the Living God, who is in the process of renewing me to right relationship with Himself. I am getting to know Him personally in a way that I have not known Him before. In the system, I had only known about Him... now I am actually getting to know Him intimately every day.

Natural thinking tells us that those outside the system are disconnected from the Body, but this is not the Truth. Those who are learning to know Him intimately are finally becoming the Body that He created us to be. Whether one is a part of the Body does not depend on where one naturally is, but on knowing the One who is the Head. If one is intimately connected with the Head, then they are connected with His Body wherever they are naturally.

I will never give Him up and return to the emptiness of religion. This is hard to understand for those who have not yet known Him outside of their religion. Those of us who are experiencing the reality of Him in our lives outside of our religion cannot help but desire for all to know Him in this wonderful Way.

CHAPTER FIVE

CONTROL AND SPIRITUAL ABUSE

Many people assume that the main reasons for people leaving the churches must be that they have had a run-in with leadership. They have been "hurt" or wounded in some way, and that is why they leave. This is one of the few reasons that church people can understand – so they assume (often wrongly) that ALL leavers are bitter or "hurt".

But this is often NOT THE CASE AT ALL. As we have seen, there are a whole raft of much deeper reasons for people leaving churches than just "problems with the leadership". However it is a factor for some leavers, especially those who have come from more "controlling" environments. Sadly, particularly amongst Pentecostals in recent years, control and spiritual abuse seem to have become more and more prevalent. It is the misuse of terms like covering, submission and authority that have often led to these problems.

A number of Out-of-church people who wrote to me highlighted the fact that leadership in the Bible often seemed quite different to much of what we see today. They also noted that some of the teachings found in today's churches were making the problem worse. Below are several emails relating to this:

From: Alistair (New Zealand):

> *I have many sincere, clear thinking and effective friends, who just do not want to be a part of the system which is called church and in most cases it is the issue of leadership. When "authoritarianism" which is not of, or from God becomes evident, the discerning know and move out. They do not leave God, they just leave a system. Human imposition never did have*

Biblical authority...

From: Jeff (New Zealand):

I believe that many Pastors require the congregation to make "them" first; i.e., to put "them" on a pedestal and if you don't then you are "in rebellion" or "can't come under authority" or have "a spirit of witchcraft" or something. I have challenged leaders that they are meant to be shepherds of the sheep God has sent them, not to Lord it over them and treat them like slaves. Many Pastors are of the opinion that the sheep are there to serve them and not the way Jesus designed it in Scripture, "feed my lambs".

In Revelation 2 verse 6, Jesus talks about the Nicolaitans and that He hated them. I understand that is the only time that Jesus said he hated anything and it's mentioned twice in Revelation 2, again in verse 15. This speaks of the control the leaders had over their people and the abuse they used. A very interesting and enlightening chapter and a warning for today. It's being exposed as the same Nicolaitan spirit right here and now.

I have spoken to many Christians over the last 6 months or so who have left churches and I have asked them the reason why. Some of the answers follow: 1) There was so much spiritual abuse/ control over us. If we did not conform to the Pastors & leaders' wishes (even if they were contrary to Scripture) then we were ignored or ostracised. We dared not question anything. 2) If we didn't tithe according to their perception of our income then again we were ignored or ostracised. They were only interested in our money. 3) It was all about the Pastors. They tried to be "superstars" and if you ran around pleasing them and agreeing with them, then you were promoted or used in ministry. They only seemed to use the ones that crawled up to them. We treated them nicely but didn't go out of our way to suck up to them or allow ourselves to be controlled by them. That meant we just sat in the pews and kept them warm and were never used in ministry at all. After a while we left. We wanted to be used by God - not just sitting in the pews. The Pastors played favourites. (Quote from a close friend who left a church after 10 years faithful service). 4) The churches speak about getting out and being active in the community (being Jesus to the world) but it ended up being a "bless me" club. Lots of talk about taking the gospel to the community in practical ways but nothing ever happened. 5) Our needs were never met. We were expected to be available to work for the church whenever they required us. But we never felt that they cared about our needs. 6) Each week was just like a performance. The Pastor up there performing to keep us coming back and keep taking our 10% income so he could keep his job. No Spirit of God anywhere.

I will finish there, I have a book full of them...

From: John (USA):

I have been in churches that emphasize "God's man of the hour" and the expected awe that was supposed to be accorded "the anointed". I heard one sermon of a renowned prophetic minister who preached that if someone served and attended to "the man of God" then the anointing of the man of God would eventually fall on the servant as in Elisha-Elijah. And there was a lot of reference to this anointed and that anointed minister, where they were held in superman status. I'm not being irreverent here because I agree with Paul on giving due respect to those who have Labored in the Lord. However some things began to stand out.... I was sensing pride, boastfulness and self glorification and not a sense of God's awe and presence.

I have heard ministers use the Scripture "Touch not the Lord's anointed" to mean that "common" Christians as well as the world had better watch the way they treat the minister. God most certainly does watch out over his own – I have seen it personally. But Christianity is not "treat me right – or else!" That is witchcraft.

- 49 -

God wants power and purity. If you were to have only one, purity would be it! Power without love and purity produces tyrants and despots intoxicated with power.

From: Mike (USA):

I have recently read several books concerning the early church and what Jesus left for us, in comparision to what we call "church" today. There doesn't seem to be any Scripture supporting a pastor driven, pastor run, pastor supported Church in the New Testament. Paul suggested a 5-fold ministry, also mentioning something about "every joint supplying..." The pastor was never intended to do "it all"!!

Others who wrote to me told of the bad experiences they had personally had with church leaders. Sadly, this is somewhat common amongst Out-of-church people. One cannot help but wonder how many Christians are being virtually driven out of churches because of terrible experiences such as these:

From: Tina (USA):

As a new believer in 1979, without any prior church background, I was led to a charismatic church with a new pastor starting out (with a Pastor's heart) and was part of that fellowship for 15 years. It was a family. I was taught the Bible. There was love... there was God in the midst of us. In 1997, without going into details... this Pastor resigned his position and moved on. A Word of Faith pastor came and took over the church and has been building a 'big ministry'... a lot of hype replaced what we had. We received a lot of teaching about honoring the 'man of God', being an Armour-Bearer, etc, etc.

My husband and I resigned our positions there and left without 'taking anyone with us'. Today, almost all of the original group is gone and not attending 'church' anywhere. Won't go into all that transpired over the three years we stayed there, but to sum it up, as I was driving down the street trying to figure out what happened, the Lord said: "You were spiritually raped."

We have tried to find different places to attend but can't seem to plug in... just can't/won't 'play the game anymore'. It gets lonely at times... you know, the Body being a many-members type of reality. No unforgiveness, resentments or bitterness in my heart... pretty sure all that has been dealt with... just a longing for pure fellowship with a community of Believers without agendas and with Jesus as the only King.

From: Larry (USA):

I came out of such a church as described in your article, very authoritative, almost dictatorial. I was in this environment for 15 years. I ended up getting excommunicated for leaving this church and nearly had a nervous breakdown in the process. In the church's view, I did not leave them, I left God, and they made that plain to me. Overcoming this, and the years of mental abuse that I received was very difficult. This took me years, so I can understand why people are conscious over a strong church authority in their lives. How many churches are Christ-like anyway? I see more of sin and the world in the church than I do of Christ. I guess I feel more comfortable guiding my own life than to have a bunch of busybodies, who are on a power trip, try and tell me what to do and how to live life. I hope you can understand that. Sometimes I think only a person who has gone through something like this can understand what it's like to be under the authority of an abusive pastor for a long time.

From: April (USA):

I am an "out-of-church" Christian; part of a charismatic fellowship for 13 years that was heavily into "reconstructionist theology" including worship of leadership as "God's anointed" and required "discipleship/submission to authority" (which amounted to slave-labor for all authority figures and things like having to ask permission to visit my parents or friends outside

- 51 -

the church).

I finally left that church in 1987 and, believe it or not, came away with a few good things: scholarly inductive Bible study habits, spiritual warfare skills, intercessory prayer and body ministry practice, and contemplative worship.

I didn't join another fellowship until about 1990, when my husband and I joined an Episcopal church whose priest was charismatic... Eventually, church politics (people being motivated by greed and selfish ambition rather than by the Spirit) led me and my husband to leave this fellowship in about 1995. I no longer attend a church, though my husband now attends a Vineyard Christian Fellowship.

For the first few years "out of church" I felt like I was doing something wrong, but every time I asked the Lord if I should be attending somewhere else, He said no. So, for the past 8 years I have been cultivating relationships with my neighbors and loving and praying for them. I have had many opportunities to share the love of Jesus with them.

When I feel safe enough, I want to resume fellowship with a local body of believers.

From: Sherril (South Africa):

I love the Body of Christ but I have become so disillusioned with leaders. I am praying for God to place me in a Body where the leaders have integrity.

My recent experiences have been with men who are not interested in the "sheep" at all. They have been left to fend for themselves. The pastoring has been left to lay people like myself. Three pastors that I know have been involved with dishonest money dealings.

I cannot tell you how this has distressed me. These men are all

- 52 -

still in the ministry and I just see more brokenness and scattering of the sheep. I have even considered starting my own church. I have a Bachelors Degree in Theology and will start work on my Masters shortly. I know that I would have to have very clear leading by the Holy Spirit, but that is how desperate I have become.

From: Dennie (USA):

I worked in a Christian store and what I saw there broke my heart. I tried really hard to remember that Christians are still works in progress but my heart became so heavy I had to quit or be consumed with brokenness. My church is wonderful but it is filled with factions with different visions who want their way. For 5 months I have withdrawn from contact with church and Christians and my heart hurts.

From: Nate (Australia):

My wife and I were in the band and leadership of a 200-strong Pentecostal church. My thoughts at the time and afterward are that the pastors were very controlling. We were encouraged to play and speak in a way which appealed to people's emotions – this was interpreted as being Spirit-led. I (personally) felt that I was being manipulative, and manipulated. My wife and I felt rather disillusioned by the fact that the pastor's focus seemed resolutely on increasing numbers, and finding the "perfect" building. Time and again the preaching centered around this topic. Other things were preached, but the sole purpose of the Sunday service seemed to be (in my eyes) to manipulate people into becoming "passionate" about the "building" and whatever the latest "move" was.

My wife and I felt so compromised and time-deprived, so we finally went to the pastors and said we wanted to take a break from the band and leadership. This wasn't taken as we'd hoped, and we got into a big fight where words such as "deceived" and "divisive" were thrown at us.

I think at this stage I became dispensable. The pastors concentrated their efforts on my wife, trying to "win" her back. They told her that I was just rebelling and other things – that they'd had dreams, etc. – which made me even more angry when she told me. I was resolute in my decision, which made my wife feel like she was being pulled in two directions. (At this stage we were still going to the church, and everyone was pretending that nothing had happened). Finally we moved town – which cut our ties with the pastors...

From: G.F. (Location unknown):

I long for discipleship, accountability, loving correction, and meeting together more than just Sundays... But my ability to trust my leaders also was so maimed by my vulnerability over issues in my personal life and resultant rejection, not once but repeatedly... then severely taken advantage of by another highly visible "Man of God". So I have opted out of the system... I desire to know the Lord, but I don't know if I will ever be willing to risk the BIG Church again. Fortunately, I have friends in the same boat and we gather to love The Lord and each other.

From: Lynda (USA):

Our story.... We helped build and pay for a church building. Laid our lives down for over 20 years, serving in every way.... Led with a team for a while (though not papered). After 20+ years we brought in a pastor and his wife from a local "denomination" – they annihilated us – slander – railing – spiritual abuse... Almost everyone that was there when they took over was forced out - one man tried to commit suicide over the horridness of their actions toward us all.... long story short – took 2 years – in a cave – to heal. We thought the Lord was finished with us.... and I personally was afraid to ever see another "Christian" – they had slandered me so badly.... Then – the Lord started over... and we realized it was HIM all along... He drop-kicked us over the goal post of the religious system –

*we died and then we were resurrected.... NOW we are living –
really living in FREEDOM – no abuse or religious programs
and control – no hierarchical / political garbage... Being Jesus
on the earth... loving, honoring people.... not building for the
glory of man.... But to glorify Jesus. We are a safe place!!*

*Our new ministry... We started in our home – outgrew it and
now meet in a conference center for worship.... We are so
thankful that the Lord got us out of that system – men building
kingdoms for their own name and glory, etc... And just in case
you are wondering – we have forgiven and rejoice in our
beloved enemies that were used by God to bring us deliverance.*

One woman who wrote to me put it very eloquently when she
posed a series of questions aimed at the very heart of the modern
church:

From: Lynnette (USA):

*When did we stop being a hospital for sinners? When did we
become a sanctuary for saints? When did the spirit of control
become the head of the church? Where did the Spirit of the Lord
go?*

*How long Oh Lord must this go on? A fire burns deep within
those that are wandering outside the church. When God?
When?*

*I am wandering in this place like an outcast, but I remember,
Oh dear Lord I remember when You moved. I pray for the day
when I can see You move again in the places that are Yours.
Church as usual has become a very cold, dead, dry place no
matter what the title of the church is. When do we stop playing
church and start being the Body and Bride?*

CHAPTER SIX

THE MACHINE

A large number of the people who wrote to me mentioned how tired they had become of all the programs, church-growth techniques, building-funds and systems found in today's churches. "Where is God in all of this?" was a common cry. To them, it is almost as though the church has become a kind of 'machine' that grinds on and on, whether God is present or not. For many, this was a significant factor in their decision to pull out of the churches. In fact, quite a few of those who wrote had been former leaders who had fully participated in this "machine" themselves:

From: D.O. (USA):

Your "Out of Church Christians" article really grabbed me. I also read the other testimonies of people who were tired of the church "game." I wonder how many testimonies you will hear from Pastors like myself who also got tired of the church game, didn't know what to do about it, and when I prayed, there was great silence in Heaven (as well as on my part of the earth) so I quit!!

I pastored Foursquare churches fifteen years and an Assembly of God for eight. I finally got tired of pouring my heart out to people who just didn't seem to "get it." Oh, there were some with a good degree of zeal, but they went right off to Bible school and became ministers in their own right. This is not bad, but it left me with no one to help me. We had "glorious song services", exciting prophecies, messages in tongues, testimonies, special singers and all the rest - but it didn't seem to have any lasting effect on anybody. If we should have a rather dull service following one of the "glorious" ones, people were ready to leave.

I just got tired! Tired of trying to get people "fired-up" for Jesus. Tired of trying to help them get out of sinful and self-destructive practices. Tired of crying my eyes out when people, in spite of my efforts would go off into fornication, adultery, drugs or whatever. I even got tired of not having my prayers answered regarding these people.

I also got tired of taking care of old church buildings in need of repairs. Air-conditioning and/or furnaces breaking down. Tired of my wife having to spend hours doing the janitor work. I was also tired of her having to drive all the church "poor" folk all over town to get their chores done.

I got tired of paying the bills and keeping the Tax-man happy by obeying all the IRS rules for churches that in reality "hamstring" a church. I got tired of a denomination that charges its ordained clergy per month to retain their credentials.... I got so tired I quit my church and my denomination. I was frustrated, angry and hurt – and a little disappointed in God Himself for not doing something to keep his churches from being so lax spiritually, and so materially-minded.

I didn't go to church anywhere for over a year. Finally at my wife's persistant urging we started "checking-out" churches in the area. I don't need to go into details to talk about what was going on there. Other writers have eloquently described the endless preoccupation with the various "activities" to keep everyone busy and/or happy.

Recently the Lord has been nudging my heart to get ready to minister again. I don't think that the Lord wants me to be a "pastor of a church" as we know it now. It may be a home Bible study - I just don't know....

From: Phil (Australia):

As an ex-Pastor of a Pentecostal assembly (in NZ) I saw firsthand the inside workings of a large movement, and left disappointed, rejected, disturbed, dismayed and many other "dis" words. Now many years later I am free and healed of all that, but as far as Churches themselves and those that run them is concerned, not much has changed.

Most churches and Pastors (not all) are primarily interested in their "success". This success is of course measured by the size of the congregation and they feel the need to validate their existence as the "head of the team". Big church = big success syndrome.

That in itself has problems enough, but even more disturbing is the imperative to be constantly "flag waving" as extolling the virtues of their particular movement. Often they see themselves as having something unique, exclusive or some other special call or revelation of God that the others don't - thus setting themselves up as proud, and sometimes boastful. "Hey, we're special, we're doing what others aren't or can't" (even thought they may not actually be doing anything out of the ordinary).

As a nationwide body of believers we've done precious little over the last few decades other than keep the doors open. Many Churches by and large are predictable, often irrelevant, frequently boring even. I get so sick of preachers and Pastors raving on about the awesome presence of God in the place, the strong anointing that's here, when in reality, there's little more than a lot of hot air coming from the front....

From: Anthony (USA):

I eventually found myself in what some call a Holiness Pentecostal church. We spent many years there trying to do what was right. I even got a degree from one of the organization's Bible Colleges.

- 59 -

As time passed we left this organization to work with other churches, some independent, some parts of other organizations (Assemblies of God, Vineyard, etc.) We saw some good and bad in each but overall we were never satisfied... it was as though the depth we wanted in God was not really there, so much of what we found in the churches was really superficial. Many churches proclaimed they did not believe in "programs" but their very non-program was a program in itself from which they could not deviate. As much as it pains me to say it, what we observed was Jesus being pushed out of the churches and plans and programs of man being placed IN the churches. It seemed as though church was not about the Lord at all but about "church" and the pastor or his ministry...

From: Teresa (USA):

We were strong Church leaders. Between my husband and I we taught teens, kids ministry, worship, poor ministry, jail ministry, lay counseling, intercession, prophetic groups, small group ministries, and my favorite which was women's ministry.

We were involved in this Church from late 1990 until late 1999 so we certainly would not be considered "Church hoppers" but dedicated to the things of the kingdom. Why we left you might ask? As the Church grew, programs became more important than people. People began to be declined ministry positions if they didn't dress a certain way, talk a certain way, or jump through all of the "hoops" that they desired. I began to be a thorn because I went to battle for multiple people that were not "allowed" to do ministry. They had no scriptural reasons or integrity issues to keep them from doing tasks in the Church. I tried to respect their decisions and be under the authority God has placed there, but it got more difficult as time went...

I had a scrapbooking party a few days ago and realized that except for one Church attender, I had a room of 15 additional women who had been hurt by the Church and bailed. These are good women who instead of continuing in their search of Jesus, they stopped because the Church has told them that they are no longer "good enough" because they also do not buy the stuff that is being taught...

From: Mario (Canada):

The fact that there is such a large and growing number of true Christians who share a deep rooted frustration about the established "Church System" could be viewed as an indication that God Himself is the Author of that frustration.

The following is my own, personal experience... It was in 1993 when I was asked to take part in a church plant. After about five years I found myself burdened with an ever increasing frustration concerning church stuff. While the congregation kept rapidly growing, our progressive church leaders began to implement more and more strategies and programs to ensure the continued success of the ministry.

As a member of the worship team I had to spend hours at seminars and in meetings. The objective was to develop a most efficient, cutting-edge ministry. We had to learn all about the meta church system and how to create a comfortable atmosphere in a user-friendly environment. And, while strategically focusing on peoples needs, to be "seeker sensitive" was seen as the key for church growth and success.

It was during that time that I became convinced that "seeker sensitive" really means being a people pleaser. Soon I found myself wrestling with a spirit of guilt and condemnation. Maybe I was just too critical or judgemental in my attitude. But, no matter how hard I tried to calm my convictions, the frustration that I felt was only increasing. Trying to talk about it wasn't going anywhere, and praying for the church leadership didn't seem to help either.

Finally, after the Lord had given me a vision regarding the root of the problems in our church, I decided that I could no longer play this game. In the vision that led to my decision I saw a picture of a boardroom. God had called for a meeting where He told the pastors of our church that He was giving them a ministry, and that they would be meeting together on a regular basis. The Lord wanted to help and equip them with everything they needed. So they kept meeting until one day our pastors told Him that they don't want to bother Him with these meetings any longer. They felt confident that they had now learned how to successfully run the church, and that, with all of the acquired study materials, the seminars and courses, they would be able to do just fine.

Although the church continued to grow in numbers, many quality people have left in their quest to find His glorious presence rather than another program or tradition. In their wilderness, they have developed an unquenchable thirst for His water of life.

Others who wrote to me declared their frustration at having seen man-made methods and programs take over something that is supposed to be a haven of spiritual refreshing – with a focus on GOD moving and not MAN. Many of them had seen so much of this kind of thing that they had almost despaired of finding a place where God was truly free to move:

From: Connie (USA):

It is hard to sit in an institution that professes to be serving the Father, when all around you watch and "see" the things of man on the rise more and more. I couldn't stay in that place anymore. I would find myself warring in the spirit before I even got to the building and praying for answers from the Lord. There are so many programs being brought in. I heard prayers like, "Father, I pray that everyone here will come up under these new programs and be a team player, and if they don't then get them out of my church." That one broke something in me that I can't explain. My spirit was in sorrow and pain. I cried out, Oh God, Oh God, Oh God.

It is very sad when you see how the "church" has become a thing, an "it". It has a bank account and people are sought to become members to take care of all the bank loans. Then they want to make the building bigger so we can house the new members they are out to bring in. IF it was for the Lord, that would be great. But I find it hard to find God anywhere involved or seen. Your article was right when you stated, WHERE IS GOD IN TODAY'S CHURCH?

From: Robin (USA):

I have not found a church. I have attended churches in a 30 mile radius and have not found one who has the heart of God. For the most part, they are about money. One does not allow you to minister in any way unless you prove that you tithe 10% (not just say, but PROVE). What happens to the ones who cannot tithe because to do so would make their family starve?

From: Lisa (New Zealand):

Oh, how one could go on forever, about why so many truly Born-again Christians have and are continuing to leave the physical church... When one really takes a cold hard look at the institution of church in the West this is precisely the problem, ITS an INSTITUTION. The problem for me is, it is no different to the strict Italian Catholic upbringing I received as a child. How embarrassing it was to realize that they are all the same, they all run the same.

From: Tony (South Africa):

In the early 90's the era of the mega church started here in South Africa. Even the local mainstream denominational churches were swept up and many adapted the cell church system with the many trappings and promises of success that the system offered. A few of the charismatic leaders in the nation had in fact applied the systems with great success and built mega churches, which these churches amplified as being the blessing of God, which even made worldly peoples' mouths hang open at the extravagance of the churches in their buildings, etc. And the extravagant lifestyle of the leaders, but this was all toted as "Blessing from God" and the show goes on.

"Excellence" was the buzzword and everybody was striving to achieve this with bigger worship bands and glossier pamphlets. Enough just never being enough, some leaders even had more than one church and so became self-appointed apostles with titles like founder and President of whatever ministries. These Apostles gaining this newfound importance which needed to be propped up even more and security guards were now employed to protect "The man of God", while he arrogantly strutted around like a peacock with little or no touch of reality, never mind even being in touch with God.

These churches were the breeding ground for the performance-driven and they flourished in this newfound environment. At the end of the 90's the buzzword was VISION and DESTINY, with these churches having huge Visions to take their cities and their nations for God. These visions, however large, were just man's attempt to reach heaven by his own means and striving efforts. These visions, like the original Tower of Babel, have that same "come let us build for ourselves" stamp on them and sadly they have the same end result - The confusion and scattering of God's people.

This problem is as old as the church itself. It is common for man to leave the voyage of faith in grace and charter a course based on works and sadly the end is always the same. You are left with a bunch of burned out and hurt Christians, and a leader that ends up falling to the very laws he practiced and preached every Sunday. We've seen countless numbers of leaders fall to sin in mainly two categories, women and money. You see, the one thing works cannot suppress is the flesh. It is only the Son that can set us free and grace is His ability operating in our lives, not our own ability.

The thing that got my attention was the lack of God in all this activity. People never got healed, set free and had no change in their lives. They became sin conscious and spent their lives walking in guilt and condemnation. Trying the latest strategy or buying the latest book or going to seminars to try and straighten out their lives. Divorce and other social problems were as common in the church as in the world. With some of the top leaders falling in this category....

Many who wrote to me disagreed with the entire mindset of today's organized church and the way it is run. They simply do not believe it is Scriptural or right:

From: Richard (USA):

The Church of the Lord Jesus Christ is not a man made organization or institution. It never has been and it will never be so. That man attempts to organize and put his approval on God is comical at best, it is extremely tragic at worst. In the process of doing so God is eventually just pushed out of the whole picture.

From: Tom (USA):

The mainstream religious Christian today is so often caught up in doing "christian" things that they have lost sight in BEING Christian. Performing obligations imposed by religious systems does not make you a Christian - just religious and often tired and discouraged – ask the many pastors who today fit that description. The world sees this and consequently doesn't see any redeeming value in the church that attracts them.

The church systems today are so busy seeking that one formula that will bring in the masses of lost souls. They're even resorting to entertainment, complete with coffee and capuccino in the services to keep people "happy" and wanting to come back. Where's the call to repentance and humility and the call to walk without compromise? The reason is that we are more concerned about making someone feel good than we are about making someone "good" (redeemed).

I am from America, but I have a friend who lives in Australia. He shared with me a brochure handed out by a local church to the neighborhoods to attract people to their church. Nowhere in the brochure was Jesus even mentioned and all through the brochure there were pictures of kids, clowns, and people helping and being nice to people. That's all well and good as kids like having fun and people should be helping each other, but the question still stands, Where is Jesus? None of these "good" works in the community can save the soul.

"What does it profit the church to gain a church full of people, but lose every soul?"

From: Roberta (USA):

It seems to me that many of those who are "out of-church" have not only gotten tired of programs but also of church-as-a-spectator-sport. If all one is allowed to do in church is watch, they might as well stay home and watch from a distance. Even if one is "allowed to participate" in the programs, it is still a program and not God.

My heart cries and I weep with God sometimes over the spectator spirit in the church. I want so badly to be in a place where the people want God so much that they will consecrate themselves and prepare themselves for a real visitation from God and not just a good show. He will not tolerate the idolatry in the church that gives the glory to the performers.

Some had come up with an entirely different solution to the "machine" – and that was to start something themselves with a whole different flavor:

From: Bob & Jan (USA):

> *The Lord led us to a huge park in our area which is quite a gathering place for people and said to go be a presence there. Well, to make a long story short, we have been meeting with a group of people there for many months now. Since we live in Florida it is easier to meet outside. We meet under a pavillion and just recently we were offered the use of a building free to use when weather is bad, but we all enjoy the freedom of being out in His creation. It's wonderful worshipping looking up at the sky! We do not consider ourselves a church. We are the "church." We have no format or overhead. We just go and wait on God. It's so refreshing. He shows up every time. We are still growing and learning and only hope we don't get too big or start planning an agenda and end up right back where we were. We enjoy the simplicity of it. Also, part of our being there is for outreach. We hope to draw people in and also we are reaching out to people who live in the campground located on the park grounds....*

It is clear to me that this "machine" thing is a major issue to many Out-of-church believers (and rightly so). Until they see a Body that is more of an 'organism' rather than an "organization" they will simply not be interested. The programs, the activities, the fund-raising and so on – all have the smell of "MAN" about them. But what these people are desperate for is "MORE OF GOD". And until they see this in the churches, many simply won't be coming back.

CHAPTER SEVEN

WHY THE 'WILDERNESS'?

The 'wilderness' is not a concept that is understood too well in Christendom, despite the fact that it is all the way through the Bible. From the book of Genesis right through Revelation there are clear references to the 'wilderness' as being something God often employs in His dealings with men. The pattern is undeniable.

But why does God use it so often? And why is a spiritual wilderness so necessary? What is its purpose and how does it change us?

When we look through the Scriptures we see that the wilderness is often a place of spiritual "crisis" and also preparation. It is the place God sends us before the "real action" begins – before we enter into the full purposes of God in our lives. There must be 'death' before there can be resurrection. There must be a desert place before the "promised land".

The wilderness is a place of trial and testing, of brokenness and full surrender to God. The props and activities that have kept us continually striving to "make things happen" are stripped away. Our self-reliance is shattered and replaced with a total reliance on God alone. Every "idol" in our lives (often including our own ministry) is brought under the piercing searchlight of God. Our selfish motives and ambitions are shown for what they are. This process may take years. Finally we emerge broken, chastened and purified. The process has matured and cleansed us in so many ways. We are now ready for the fulfillment of all that God originally called us to do. But our heart-motives are vastly different from what they were before.

We see this pattern all the way through Scripture. Many lessons can be learned from what we read there. Let's take a look at some examples:

From what we can tell, the original patriarch Abraham went through at least two major 'wilderness' experiences during his walk with God. The first was when he and his family set out from their homeland, "not knowing where" – on the long journey to Canaan. The second instance was a major spiritual crisis in Abraham's life – where his future and everything he believed in was at stake.

God had promised Abraham a son – that he would be the "father of many nations". Yet when Isaac, the son of promise arrived, God commanded Abraham to journey to Mt Moriah and sacrifice Isaac to Him! All of Abraham's hopes and dreams were represented in that little boy, and yet here was God commanding him to kill the son of promise! This is very similar to what many people find in their own wilderness times. It is almost as if they have to put to death their own dreams and even the callings of God on their lives. Yet at the very last minute, God stayed Abraham's hand and gave him a ram to sacrifice in Isaac's place. It was Abraham's faith and total trust in God that was demonstrated that day. His willingness to sacrifice all of his dreams and hopes to God was exactly the heart-attitude that God required.

Another example from Genesis is that of Joseph – a story that has 'wilderness' written all over it. Joseph was the favored son in his family, and had been given dreams by God of his destiny as a great leader amongst his people. Yet little did he realize that the path to this destiny was one of betrayal, pain, rejection and imprisonment. In fact, an essential factor in this story was the jealousy of Joseph's brothers, who sold him into slavery in Egypt. If they had not done this, then it is doubtful that his God-given dreams would ever have come to pass. Even after Joseph got to Egypt the nightmare continued. He was thrown into jail for years, for a crime he did not commit. All this time, God was breaking him and molding him to be the great leader that he was to become. For it is only in the desolate places that God is able to do this deep preparation work.

Then all of a sudden after years and years, in one day Joseph went from prison to palace! Because of his God-given wisdom in interpreting the dreams of Pharaoh, Joseph was made Prime Minister over all Egypt – second only to the king. His years of waiting in the wilderness were over. A new season had begun. A season in which he would see every promise that God had given him fulfilled.

Probably the best-known instance of a 'wilderness experience' in the Old Testament is the story of Moses and the children of Israel. There are some important lessons in this one as well. We all know the story. Moses had been raised and trained all his life in the palaces of Egypt. But when he came face-to-face with his heritage as an Israelite, he rose up "in his own strength" and killed an Egyptian slave-driver. He was then forced to flee into the desert, where he was to spend 40 YEARS as a simple shepherd in the wilderness. What an enormous length of time! Imagine if every Christian leader had to spend that long in the wilderness before God would allow them to lead His people! It is almost impossible to imagine the depths of despair and "death" to all his dreams and hopes that Moses went through during this time. In fact, after 40 years it is hard to imagine anyone being "deader" to the usual ambitions and temptations of leadership than Moses would have been. And what PATIENCE these years of waiting must have produced in him!

Again we see here the lengths that God will go to in the "preparation" phase of a leader (though 40 years is unusually long). The isolation, the chafing, the crying out to God for deliverance – all play their part. Such an experience is almost irreplaceable. That is why God uses it so often. The hearts of driven men are so similar in so many ways, that God's "cure" becomes similar also! He will even shut us up in a kind-of 'prison' for a time so we cannot escape the process. It is that important. He does not want 'self'-oriented leaders shepherding his precious sheep.

After his 40 years of preparation, Moses returned to Egypt at God's command to lead His people out of bondage. This was the beginning of the entire nation of Israel's wilderness experience. For when they left Egypt the only way to their "Promised Land" was through the desert. Some commentators say that in a straight line, their journey could have taken just a few weeks or less. But because of their disobedience and fear, the vast majority of those who left Egypt were destined to die in the desert, never reaching the Promised Land. In fact, their wilderness journey ended up taking 40 years!

Now we need to take special note of this fact: Not everyone who entered the wilderness survived it. In fact, multitudes perished there. The wilderness tried them and found them wanting. They went to the place of testing and failed the test. This is a pretty crucial fact to realize in our day also. Just because we are "called out" and enter a wilderness time, does not mean that we will embrace the dealings of God and respond appropriately. It is entirely possible to lose everything out there. These people lost out completely. Only their children came through to inherit the promises of God.

Centuries later we read of another pivotal leader in Israel's history – who also endured a very long and trying 'wilderness' process. This was David – the shepherd who was destined to be king.

David spent years literally running for his life from Saul, the existing king of Israel, who felt jealous and 'threatened' by David. The young man knew he was called to be king, but it was through great tribulation that he would come into the kingdom. David spent years hiding in caves and even in the villages of the Philistines to escape the envy of King Saul. 400 other outcasts joined themselves to him, so he had his own small army of 'rebels' to lead. God was training him to be a good leader. But it was a terribly taxing and frustrating period of his life.

You see, God could not afford to have another 'Saul' leading Israel. That is why he had to test and try David to such a degree. He wanted to ensure that he was a man "after God's own heart". This process took years and years.

One of the key tests that David faced was the test of "rebellion". At one time he had the opportunity to take the life of Saul very easily, and his men urged him to do so. If he killed Saul the kingdom would be his. But David would not raise his hand against Saul. He still regarded him as the "Lord's Anointed", even though it was clear that Saul had been rejected by God as king. David would not move to bring about his own destiny by chopping down the existing leadership. He would wait for God's hand and God's perfect time. This was a crucial test for David.

Eventually, when Saul was killed in battle, David did indeed come into the kingdom at precisely God's appointed time. Thus began a "golden age" in the history of Israel. And David's lengthy time of preparation in the wilderness stood him in great stead right to the end of his life.

But the Old Testament makes it clear that it was not just future kings or leaders that God trained in the wilderness. Most of God's prophets were usually prepared for their ministry in these places of isolation and desolation as well. Every would-be Elijah or Elisha of God must go through such times of intense spiritual training. And this is true not just of the Old Testament but also of the New. In fact, to this day, if there is one type of ministry that is most associated with the concept of 'wilderness' it is the "Prophetic" ministry. And I believe that there is a strong 'prophetic' aspect to a lot of what we are seeing with the Out-of-church movement today.

We could give examples of 'wilderness' experiences for many of the Old Testament prophets, for this seemed to be almost a universal thing that they went through. But I think that one of the most interesting prophets to look at is John the Baptist, the prophet who 'prepared the way' for the New Testament era. Jesus declared that, "Among them that are born of women there has not risen one greater than John the Baptist." For John had always been destined to be a prophet – filled with the Holy Spirit from his mother's womb. And yet, after thirty years of preparation, the duration of his ministry was to be only six months! But what a six months it was.

John the Baptist was truly a 'wilderness' prophet in the most radical sense. During his preparation and training time we are told that he was hidden in the desert places until the time of his showing-forth came. Suddenly he arrived, as if from nowhere, with a piercing word of repentance on his lips. His sermons were amongst the most fiery of any prophet in history. "And there went out unto him all the land of Judea, and they of Jerusalem, and were all baptized of him in the river of Jordan, confessing their sins" (Mk 1:5).

Not only were John's days of preparation based in the desert, but his entire ministry as well! He was a wilderness man in every way. And it was he who had the honor of baptizing Jesus – the promised Messiah.

It is important to remember that Jesus too went through a wilderness period just before His ministry began. As we all know, after he was baptized the Holy Spirit descended upon Him like a dove. "Then was Jesus led by the Spirit into the wilderness to be tempted by the devil" (Mt 4:1). This wilderness period was a time of testing and trial, of fasting for 40 days and nights, and of relentless attacks from the enemy. When Jesus had made it through to the other end, He was truly ready to begin His ministry. Thus, even in the life of the Savior of the world, the 'wilderness' was a crucial milestone.

The apostle Paul was another one whom God required to go through such an experience. He records that immediately after being converted and filled with the Holy Spirit, he spent time in Arabia (a desert region) communing with God and did not visit the apostles in Jerusalem for at least three years (Gal 1:17-18). This again illustrates how important it is for those with a special message from God to spend time alone with Him before showing themselves to the world. They must be made ready first. And that is what the wilderness is all about.

As we have seen, all the way through Scripture many of God's future leaders and spokesmen were sent into a place of aloneness and brokenness before being brought into their true destiny. We have not even mentioned heroes of God such as Noah, Joshua, Jacob, Job and others who all had similar experiences. Part of this process lies in the "waiting" that takes place. Also, the fact that all the supporting 'props' are taken away. The waiting alone can be torture.

The wilderness also deals with any fear of man or 'systemized' way of looking at things. God often uses it to bring a whole fresh perspective, which is very important for leaders who are going to be representing a "new" approach or facing opposition because of the confrontational words that they are bringing. The lonely desert years give them backbone to stand up to the crowd or the powers-that-be, and declare God's truth without compromise. They now truly fear God rather than man. And they think differently from others. The wilderness is vital for anyone who is wanting to bring fresh manna to God's people.

Below are a number of interesting emails I received relating to this topic:

From: Scott (USA):

We're quick to equate "The Wilderness" to a negative thing. I don't believe that. I believe that some of what God is getting ready to do, some of it can't be taught from the pulpit. The old expression, "It can't be taught, it has to be caught" plays a large part of this.

"And the child grew, and waxed strong in spirit, and WAS IN THE DESERTS till the day of his showing unto Israel" (Lk 1:80). There was an order change getting ready to happen... John the son of Zacharias was not going to learn that TRUTH in his father's home, nor in church on the Sabbath. It was a revelation that came while John was in the wilderness. What God was getting ready to do, the move of God that was getting ready to unfold (Jesus) had to be taught somewhere outside of the influence and the order of that day.

I believe there is an order change coming to the church today, just like in the days of John. I don't mean some new order of salvation or grace. I mean in the church. We've produced a lot of stuff that Jesus didn't have anything to do with. I believe the change of order will bring God's order back to His people. And I believe that God has those that He calls sons in those "wilderness" places because He's getting ready to impart and deposit something into their hearts that quite possibly can't be taught in the church today...

I'm not saying that the church is all screwed up. I love the church. I attend every week. I believe those in the wilderness love the church as well. I believe they are there at the prompting of the Holy Spirit. There are things and truths that God is opening them up to that can't be taught within the 4 walls of the church right now.

In your article, you mentioned that "thousands are already opting out. And many feel like they are 'waiting' for something." I believe that! I believe they're there with expectation. Fasting, praying, listening for the voice of God. I doubt many of them even understand why. But just by gut level faith, they believe Jesus has said, "Come away."

You mentioned that it's not possible for them to stay away forever. Agreed. I believe they will return and infiltrate the church. And bring with them a message and a revelation that will stagger us.

Obviously, there are those who will use "hurts, wounds" as reasons to walk away and not be responsible. Others are just plain lazy and carnal. But there are those who have heard the voice of the Master compelling them to seek his face and his heart outside the 4 walls of the local church.

From: Deborah (Location unknown):

Many have left the 'system' and don't know why. In Egypt there

- 76 -

were great demands on the Jewish people to 'work'. This is symbolic of the weariness that comes with 'works'. Performance based righteousness is extremely exhausting. Most have bought into the system unconsciously. I believe that God is calling many out from this 'belief system'... He is calling us out of 'Egypt'...

When He calls us 'outside the camp' it is celebration time. Why? I believe it is because He says it is time for deeper relationship with Him and for preparation. Preparation for what we are to face up ahead. The call outside the camp, just like it was for Jesus, is for us to die. It will be the best of times and the worst of times. The best of times because we get to have a deeper more real relationship than ever before with Him and be less bound by 'works'. The worst of times because what is not of Him must die. Ouch.

From: Hari (Australia):

Like many others, I am sure, we have been warned of the precariousness of being in this situation of being 'alone' and therefore subject to being set upon by wolves (although sadly I have met more of the wolves within the church) and of 'forsaking the gathering together' of the brethren.

The wilderness is a place void of distractions and pomp and fanfare, a place where the Lord alone awaits you. It has been 5 years to date and during that time we have attempted to 'get back in' but somehow we keep getting shoved 'right back out'.... We are not embittered, we are not unsubmitted but we are disillusioned.

You have to sometimes be on the outside to actually see what is going on. To be of help to a man trapped in the pit you have to be outside in order to pull him out. Of course being 'outside' is in itself an open sore to those 'inside'. It brings to the surface many questions that simply will not lay down, that do not want to be faced.

But in this wilderness we have found Him and He alone has led and fed us and caused us to grow in such a way that a thousand lifetimes of church meetings could never achieve. Perhaps like John the Baptist we are all awaiting a call to come out and go into the cities (Lk 3:2) and like him we will be a people prepared to prepare the way for His coming... Perhaps then the world will see something different, perhaps then we will once again be a people that 'turn the world upside down'.

Many of those who wrote to me had some very interesting things to say about their own 'wilderness' experience:

From: Christopher (USA):

I was mentored by two large ministries and by 1996, became second in command of a ministry here that became a known entity in prophetic circles.

By late 1999, the Lord began speaking to me about idolatry to ministry. This was very hard for me because I had simply followed the "how-to's" of my mentors and had also given up a successful career in corporate USA to answer the "call" (as I had been taught). Then in November of 2000, the Lord Himself came to me and began a dialogue...

I was sitting in my blue office recliner behind the desk when suddenly I heard the voice of the Lord begin to speak to me in a very pronounced fashion. He said, "Chris, would you be OK if I told you that we are going to take a trip to the backside of the desert and in that place, all of what you have come to think of and know as normal will cease. There will be no meetings, no activity, no visibility. It will seem as if everything has come to a stop – but – what you will have is my manifest Presence." There was a brief moment of silence at this point and then He came back to me and said, "Chris, if all you have is Me and Me alone, would I be enough for you?"

As soon as Jesus finished asking this question, I immediately knew that the right answer was "Yes" but something in me prompted me to stop and think about the question and not answer hastily. It was as if what I said was going to prophesy what would happen – and it would be set in motion immediately after I spoke it. For a brief moment, I contemplated what a "No" answer would be saying ("No, Jesus, You would not be enough. We desire the ministry more than we desire You") but this was so ludicrous that I was ready to answer His question even though there might have been a twist to it that I had not thought about. I knew that any ministry worth engaging in MUST always begin with and end with Jesus. So, I said "Yes Lord, You alone would be enough". There was another moment of silence and then He simply said, "OK". The intensity of His Presence left and I did not experience another visitation like this again until the end of June 2002.

One morning near the end of June 2002, I was sitting in exactly the same chair in my office working and the Lord again came to me as He had last November. Although it had been several months since the last "meeting", He spoke to me as if we were still engaged in our last conversation. He said, "Chris, if I had given you the things you thought you wanted in ministry, you would have come to despise them even more than you despised the aspects of business that you felt were competing for your time and hindering My call on your life – making it difficult for you to walk out what I had called you to do."

.... He said, "In the coming days, My people's greatest desire will be just to sit at My feet and enjoy sweet fellowship with Me. No longer will they have their passions wrapped around the things they do for Me. I will be their greatest passion. Then, I will say to this one, will you go and deliver this message to this group, and I will say to that one, will you go and help this one on the street who is in great need, and I will say to another, will you go and encourage this one who is My sheep. Because of their passion for Me, they will have no desire to leave their

*place at My feet but they will do as I ask out of their great love
for me. They will all go and complete their assignments exactly
as I instructed, but when they have completed what I told them
to do, their only desire will be to quickly return to their place,
sitting at My feet. Never again will they displace their passion
for Me to those things that they do for Me. I alone will be their
passion."*

*We have "come out" and I don't see us going back. And, I look
forward to seeing what the Lord will now do because I do
believe He is the One behind all this.*

From: Nancy (USA):

*I have to say that I don't feel like I'm in a wilderness. Maybe I
am and I just don't know it (ha). To me, wilderness is
somewhere where God is not there. I don't feel that way at all. I
talk to Him every day. He talks to me every day. I'm following
Him to the best of my ability. I'm trusting Him to bring me into
greater faithfulness to Him, greater dedication to prayer,
greater love for Him. Sure, I love fellowship with people, but I
had fellowship with people all the years I was in church. The
only thing missing was God!*

From: Rodney (USA):

*About 7 years ago I began to realize that I had spent my whole
life as a so-called Christian living in some kind of sin or
another thinking the whole time that I knew God. I suddenly
realized my great need of Him. I begged Him for six months to
do something for me. One day He did. In a moment he came and
cleansed me and completely redirected my life. At that time I
began to wonder why after so many years in the church I had
never seen that kind of power. Loving God more than ever and
yet growing more and more detached from the organized
church. I have struggled with guilt, extreme loneliness, many
almost sleepless nights and many other emotions because for
several years I felt like I was the only one that felt this way. Let*

me emphasize, my love for God continuing to grow this whole time. He personally teaching me things that I never learned in the church. God had filled my heart with so many wonderful things and I so much wanted to tell people, and yet there just were not ears to hear.

The wilderness has been sometimes excruciating for my family and I. It was much easier in the old days living in ignorance, just playing the game. Many times we have thought maybe we just need to go back and get involved. When we go to a "church service" we are often overcome with grief or great sadness. In the last couple of years we have been meeting other people like us and now have fellowship with a dozen or so families like ourselves and know of many more. We do from time to time attend a church service simply because we feel such a love for people that we never had before and we want to be with them (even people we don't know), yet sometimes it takes a week or so to recover from the trauma. I might add, the church we are affiliated with, as far as churches go, is probably about as good as they come.

After now going through this for 7 or so years, I would not trade it for anything. Even in the tremendous wilderness and lonely times I was so sure that it was God doing all this that I would have bet my life on it. He has been so incredibly faithful and it seems now that we are out of the wilderness and we feel something is ready to happen.

From: Nikki (USA):

Sometimes when you're alone, knowing of none or a few others - you do think you must be rebellious – but the times with God are so rich, deep and the growing roots so good – you know something about this is right. We are learning to hear, walk with and follow our Lord – in a very real and personal way. He has His reasons – and I know that I know – we will have no trouble hearing Him when He tells us to "March" – but it will probably not be into a building - but into a living temple of His children – each obeying a call they hear....

From: Donna (USA):

I have been out of the church for several years – I occasionally visit somewhere – but I always hear by the voice of the Spirit, "No – this is not your home." I have known for quite a while that my Father has had a purpose in this wilderness experience and I will understand in due time. Lately I have come to understand that it is in the desert that the highway is prepared...

I do not know exactly what my Father has planned for me,but it is something far beyond anything I can imagine. I do know that there is a revelation of restored truth that is coming to many in the desert that soon will be released. All should be making the purchases of Revelation 3:18, particularly the eye salve. Not all things come by grace-there is a price to be paid by those who would overcome.

From: Shearon (USA):

Politics doesn't belong in the church, choirs on parade don't belong in the church, hat day doesn't belong in the church, etc. We have gotten away from what the church is all about. Lord take us back.

I too have gone through a wilderness experience so I can relate to what they are going through. The wilderness isn't easy, we should all have one. The wilderness has a purpose, I thank God for my experience, I learned so much. But yes, you are right, there is a time to come out. You can't stay in the wilderness (yes, I wanted to). There is a time when God will send you out, like He did with Moses and His Son. It may be 40 days, it may be 6 months, or it may be 40 years, but you must come out. If not, what was it for?

CHAPTER EIGHT

THE DANGERS

As we have seen throughout this book, many Out-of-church people have very good reasons why they have left the churches. However, there is another side to this. For I have personally met a number of Out-of-church people who have now spent well over a decade completely outside everything. And they are out there still. Unless there is some incredibly good reason for this, I just cannot believe it is right. Sometimes a real tendency develops to just "drift along", year after year. I believe there are big dangers in this. My heart goes out to these people in their journey, but I am sometimes reminded of the children of Israel who came to love the desert more than the Promised Land – and ended up living their whole lives there. They never inherited the Land of Promise. Their home became the wilderness and they never came into their calling at all. (I am not so much addressing those in the house-churches here, but rather those at the more 'lonely' extremes).

I cannot believe that God sends us into the wilderness to live the rest of our lives there. That makes no sense – and it is totally unscriptural. The wilderness has always been a place of preparation. If we stay there too long, just because it has become 'comfortable', then we are in great danger of missing God's ultimate calling and everything He has for us. The wilderness is a place of training, not a Land of Promise.

Yet I know a large number of Out-of-church people who seem to have adopted a 'wilderness' mentality. They have become "comfortable" there, and it seems it would take the most terrible shaking for them to even consider moving. Their whole mentality makes it awfully hard for them to ever join in with anything again – even a true move of God. They have become chronic "non-joiners". Just like the children of Israel, they see the "risks" as too great. The wilderness has become their comfort zone.

I think it is especially significant that with the Israelites, their ultimate moment of crisis came when it was time to leave the wilderness and actually enter into the Promised Land. They couldn't bring themselves to do it. The risks seemed too great. I believe that this represents a moment of great danger for today's wilderness-dwellers also. For if they have been out for some years, then it becomes risky even to think of joining anything again – even a "new wineskin". I have noticed that for some, even contemplating a 'Body' environment challenges their comfort zone and they shrink back from any involvement with anything at all. It's a terrible shame. For that was the moment when the children of Israel lost everything – their entire future.

A 'wilderness' that goes on and on – for year after year – without a 'Promised Land' is a nightmare. It is proof that something is very wrong. People who become comfortable in this kind of environment need to face up to themselves. Something is definitely not right.

You see, the New Testament knows only one kind of Christianity – and that is the 'Body' kind. There is absolutely NO SUCH THING as an individualistic "leave-me-alone-by-myself" type of Christianity in the Bible. There may be wilderness periods, but these do not last forever. They are temporary. They are training and preparation times. They are not the "norm". In fact, they are nothing like normal church life at all.

I have studied Revival history, and I tell you, there has never been a Revival that involved "going off and being by yourself". Revival by its very nature is a CORPORATE thing. It is the 120 in the Upper Room, praying and fasting for days on end "in one accord". It is 3000 people coming to Christ in one day. It is Pentecost all over again. It is unity and love and ingathering. It is the very opposite of separate individualism.

Now, I have no problem with a time of preparation where

'aloneness' and separation become the norm for awhile. This may certainly occur in the lead-up to a Revival. But if it goes on and on, and becomes a "comfort zone", then I get very alarmed. Revival will never come to a bunch of rabid individualists. Such a thing is diametrically opposed to all the principles of the New Testament. For the New Testament is all about "ONE BODY" – knitted together, unified in one accord.

I am very aware that the churches we see around us today are far from being 'New Testament' churches. So I can readily understand why people hang back from joining in with them. But that is no excuse for becoming "anti-body" by nature. And I fear that this is what is happening to a lot of Out-of-church people. They are becoming chronic non-joiners. Cynics and stand-off-ish. The very opposite of 'Body' people. In fact, many are the type that will never join anything ever again. Does this sound right to you? Does this sound like a 'Revival' company? Certainly not. If you are anti-Body then you are anti-Jesus. I can't see it any other way.

As intimated earlier, I have met quite a few people (some are former leaders) who have now been Out-of-church for close to twenty years. Some of them are opposed to the whole concept of 'meetings' altogether. (Too "religious", they say). So they never really gather with any group at all. They are quite happy by themselves – "just them and God". I have to say I find this a terrible waste. I cannot help thinking of the 'unprofitable servant' who hid his talent in the ground instead of using it for God's kingdom. I cannot believe that God wants people with strong gifts and callings to spend twenty years off by themselves in some spiritual backwater, just because they no longer relate to the concept of a 'Body'. It is ridiculous. A lot of these people have insights that the church desperately needs to hear. But we will never hear them because they only ever talk amongst themselves.

There is a kind of 'elitism' (or spiritual pride) in some of this that is very distasteful. I know, because I fully partook of it myself when I was Out-of-church. It is the kind of smug attitude that says, "Church people are 'religious'. They are caught up in the 'system'.

We are free from all that. We are the ones who really know what's going on." With such attitudes it is very easy to become given-over to spiritual pride. It is no different from the Pharisees who prayed things like, "I thank you God that I am not the same as other men..."

I tell you, when my moment of "crisis" came in 1993 – the time when I came out of the wilderness – there were so many of these attitudes that God convicted me of. In fact, I came to see that there can be just as much pride and elitism and 'sectarianism' in the Out-of-church scene as in the most religious churches! When you separate yourself and look down your nose at other Christians, then you are a Pharisee. It doesn't matter whether you are In-church, Out-of-church or whatever. Self-righteousness is a terrible evil. And from what I have seen, it is rampant in many parts of this movement.

It is quite possible to be "religiously" non-religious. It is quite possible to be so frightened of anything that even looks like 'church' that you run a mile in the opposite direction and get into all kinds of silly extremes. Some of the things I have seen in the Out-of-church scene are almost laughable, if they were not so tragic. I have been in meetings where everyone was scared to be seen as too much of a "leader", so hardly anything really happened. I have been with people who felt that singing was too "religious". I have been with others who thought that anything 'organized' just could not be of God. And I have even come across some who thought that giving thanks before a meal was "religious"!

Do these people ever read their Bibles? Have they not read the Book of Acts?

You see, 'Out-of-church' can become just as much a "sect" as anything else. Unless we are careful it can become a ridiculous "anti-everything" club. It can even become our own private little "cult" – keeping us in a kind of bondage that distances us from others and prevents us from fulfilling God's purpose in our lives.

I am talking here about the 'extreme' side of this movement. But believe me, there are a lot of people caught up in this kind of thing. Let the reader beware!

Before 1993 I myself was caught up in a lot of this stuff. So what was it that opened my eyes, and brought me out of this 7-year wilderness? Quite simply, God showed me how to deal with a lot of the 'strongholds' and bondages deep within me, and as soon as they were dealt-with a whole lot of things suddenly became very clear to me. It was as if blinders fell from my eyes.

The major breakthrough came when I got a new revelation of the authority that God gives to every one of His children to "pull down strongholds" – even in their own lives. I began to see that inside of me was 'land' that had not yet been taken for God – and that was still in the hands of the enemy. There were strongholds of pride, rebellion, rejection and all kinds of bondages from the past that were deep inside me. These were not 'demons' as such, but they allowed the enemy to have footholds in my life that he could use against me. Even though I had 'repented' of a lot of things in my life, this did not seem to deal with some of these larger strongholds. Somehow they had to be rooted out.

God showed me that I needed to ask Him to shine His light on these strongholds, so it would become clear exactly what we were dealing with. I was then to RENOUNCE with my mouth, but also FROM THE DEPTHS OF MY ENTIRE BEING each of these strongholds – being very specific. I was to cast them out of myself as "unclean things" in Jesus' name – rejecting them with the full force of my entire being. It was to be a merciless "search and destroy" mission.

And it worked! Over a period of three days I went through my whole life in this way, asking God to show me anything that needed dealing with. And one by one these things were all RENOUNCED and commanded out of my life in Jesus' name. What a transformation! How my life changed in just three days!

After I had been through this process, I found that my eyes were open to a lot of things that I had thought were "OK". Some of my Out-of-church attitudes towards leadership, for instance, I now recognized as being simply 'rebellion'. And still other attitudes had clearly originated from rejection and pride, rather than anything godly. I realized that I had been just as 'religious' and smug about belonging to the Out-of-church movement as I had been earlier in my life when I belonged to a rather "exclusive" Pentecostal denomination. The attitudes were exactly the same. It is possible to be very legalistic and judgemental about being 'Out-of-church'.

But now, with these inner strongholds gone, I felt far more 'free' than I ever had before. I was experiencing true liberty in Christ – possibly for the first time. I no longer judged people by the outward form of their Christianity, or the 'boxes' they were in, but rather by their heart towards God and their sincere pursuit of Him.

I began to notice that in the Book of Acts there were STRONG LEADERS (i.e., apostles and elders) and a clear degree of ORGANIZATION AND STRUCTURE. I began to notice that there was discipline and authority (bad words in much of the Out-of-church scene). And I realized that some of my Out-of-church attitudes had been "reactions" against the present system rather than accurate Biblical viewpoints.

With realizations like these flooding my heart, my entire outlook changed and almost overnight I found that I'd left the 'wilderness' behind. It was time to come in from the cold.

So how do I view the 'Out-of-church' movement now? The fact is, I am still convinced that God is doing a preparation work in a lot of people, and so the wilderness is as important as ever. I also think that we are entering a great season of 'change' in the church. And "unlearning" the old ways to grasp hold of the new is something that God is obviously pushing. Many of the house-churches and cell-networks that are rising up are evidence of these winds of change. But there is a long way to go before we get back to the Christianity of the New Testament. This thing is only just beginning.

I am convinced that many of those who are being called out of the churches at this time have a leadership call upon their lives. In fact, I believe they may well be leaders in the coming move of God. As we have already noted, Alan Jamieson's studies revealed that a whopping 94% of the Out-of-church Christians he interviewed had been leaders of some kind in the church. That is a staggering statistic. I cannot help but think that God is about to do something new, and that He is preparing His leaders in the wilderness just as He has always done. It makes perfect sense and it is a thoroughly Scriptural concept, as we have seen.

But the fact remains that some of these people are in great danger of getting stuck in the wilderness forever. This is one of my greatest concerns. For I have seen it first-hand, and it is a terrible thing.

I am convinced that in the wilderness there are things that we HAVE to deal with if we are to make it through to the other side. This is surely one of the principal reasons that God sends us there – to deal with these issues in our lives.

As I said before, just like the children of Israel, the 'test' comes when it is time to exit the wilderness. Does rebellion or unforgiveness remain? Do problems still exist with leadership or authority? Have all the old 'wounds' been healed? Does pride or fear of rejection still hold sway in our hearts? These are crucial questions for every one of us. And they are precisely the issues that will make all the difference.

There is no denying that to come out of the wilderness is a "risk". No-one wants to get hurt again. No-one wants to be rejected again. No-one wants to have to cry 'repent' in the face of the popular crowd.

But God must have leaders. And they must be leaders He can trust. They must be leaders who are not afraid to speak out in the face of popular opinion. They must be leaders who see things 'differently' and who truly fear God rather than man. They must be good shepherds and preachers of the Truth. God must have leaders such as these. And if He has to send them to "wilderness school" and wait and wait until they are ready, then He will willingly do so. For this has always been the cost He has had to pay.

Below are some interesting emails that I received relating to all this:

From: Marilyn (USA):

I just got through reading your wilderness experience... It helped me know that I have to allow God to heal the pain I experienced at the hands of "church" people so that I can associate with them again. I was beginning to enjoy the wilderness – being by myself.

Just recently, God sent me to a conference with radical worship. I told God that He needed to tell me why I was there or I was coming home because all He had told me was that I needed to spend time with Him and I could do that just as easily at home. When I got to the conference, the speaker spoke about how important corporate worship is. God told me, 'When you were sick and dying, you spent time with me by yourself and I healed you. But now My Body is sick and dying and you must spend time with other members of My Body worshipping Me so that it can be healed.' God had told me that His Body would be healed the same way mine had been – while simply spending time with Him, enjoying His presence.

God did a major healing on my heart while I was at the conference and dredged up all the old junk. He released His Spirit into me again.

I thought I was all done with this healing stuff until today when God gave me a word that said that I needed to allow Him to heal the hurts that I had suffered. When I asked Him what these hurts were, all I kept getting were different leaders and church people. I had forgiven them and didn't have any bitterness. I didn't have a hard time asking God to bless them or to pray for them. But when it came to the idea of actually having to associate with them again, I couldn't handle that. God showed me that I had put up a big wall and separated myself because of the hurt. I even questioned if this was really from God all day because I couldn't understand why He would want me to associate with the same people who had rejected me before. A guy I know had been telling me yesterday that I needed to get in touch with several people in the area. I had absolutely no desire to. I finally told him that if God told me to I would, but I wasn't about to go to these people otherwise. Well, God started the process of telling me to do it today.

From: Mark (USA):

Remember that all the biblical people who were sent into the wilderness (Paul, Jesus, David, etc), came out of it again and rejoined the body with their newness. We all will rejoin the body too. But in rejoining, the Sauls of the old wineskin will try to resist and reject us. That is the way it always is.

God spoke to me 3 years ago (through another Christian) and He made it abundantly clear that unless I submitted to His bride, I would not be permitted to know His secrets. In the wilderness I learned volumes about Him, but last year He brought me back into the church. Of course I've found it difficult to submit to authority (having been a lone wolf for so long and having such different values). The things that God shows me in the spiritual realm, the existing churches can't really understand or perhaps they won't accept it.

This year He asked me to attend a sort of 'school' for church building – you can imagine how interesting that is, to compare their values with the values I believe God has taught me.

Yet we must always remember that David never took action

against Saul. God drew David back into the kingdom to become the new king. But all that time David had respect for God's chosen authority. I believe we must be bold enough to go forward claiming that God is doing something new, but we must also be humble enough to remember that we must submit to God's chosen authority. Although we differ to them in some ways, He did put them in places of authority.

From: Jeff (USA):

God sends us into the wilderness for a very specific time and for a very specific purpose, then He sends us back into the body of Christ to complete the work He has given us to do. God sent me into the wilderness for a time myself but that time is over now. He has since called me to a new church that believes the way I do and has begun the process of restoring to me the ministry I had before, as well as to heal my heart of some past hurts. It feels great to be a part of such a loving group that does its best to live what they profess. Part of the ministry I have now is to share those things God revealed to me during my wilderness experience. One of the things I feel led to share is how God changed "ME" during that difficult period.

This also happened to Elijah following God's victory on Mt. Carmel (I Kings 18). Remember that when he fled from the threats of Jezebel he too headed out into the wilderness for a time, and God even blessed it. But then God, after showing the man of God His glory, asked him, "What are you doing here?".... As long as Elijah remained on the "backside of the wilderness" God couldn't use him. That's why the Lord said, "What are you doing here?" and then "Go back the way you came." In other words, after God showed him what He intended to show him He sent him back to his people and back to the work of the ministry.

Also remember the wilderness is a place of testing and revelation. And, as such, it was never intended to be a permanent dwelling place for God's people... He also sends you back to share with others those things He has shown you during your wilderness experience (just as he did with me). That's why Elijah was told to both anoint Elisha as a prophet and Jehu as king. Just imagine what would have happened if he never completed that work.

From: Alison (South Africa):

I know what it is like to be in a church where my own (and my husband's) vision had long since been trampled under the feet of the leadership. And I know what it is like to wander around in the wilderness in fellowship with no one. Neither place is the Church.

I know what it is to stand in a meeting where people are being whipped up and manipulated by human emotion – and that is not the Church either.

So where is the Church? That's the point. Are "out of church" Christians actually looking for the Church – or are they content in their isolation? As long as we honestly search we are those who are ready to see truth re-born. But as soon as we are content in our isolation, adapting nicely to the wilderness and praying up "we four and no more" then, God help us, we are by our own actions delaying the return of the Lord himself.... Let's not "play" criticism any more than some "play" church.

CHAPTER NINE

THE "IN-CHURCH" OUT-OF-CHURCH

It seems that there is a tremendous groundswell of "dissatisfaction" occurring in the church right now. Could it be that God Himself may be orchestrating this, to prepare for great change and reformation amongst His people? A number of those who wrote to me are still within their churches, but are having a hard time finding good reasons to stay there. The following emails explain the reasons that many of them give for this growing dissatisfaction.

From: Noreen (South Africa):

> *I am one of those who is in but is out, if you know what I mean. I find I feel much safer with my personal relationship at home with the Lord. I also find that I am never sure about whether what is going on in the churches is right. It is awful as this evening I could have gone to church but chose not to. This leaves one feeling guiltly. However, I have never felt closer to the Lord.*

From: Candy (USA):

> *I am not "out of church" right now, but sometimes I feel like I might as well be. I went back to a Spirit-filled church that I had "joined" seven years ago. (I had gone to another Spirit-filled church for 3 years that fell apart, then went to a non-Spirit filled church off and on for 4 years). I knew I needed to get back to a Spirit-filled church.... I found out my membership had been cancelled and I needed to "rejoin" to become a member.... I still haven't done that.... I don't know why I need to. The pastor is promoting different things trying to get new members. It's not wrong, it's just that if we had true revival, people would come on their own, right? Anyway, I am struggling to keep going,*

even though I know I need to. I feel like I am in a very dry place, including when I am in church. For every person who is "out of church"... there is probably at least one "in church" who wonders why he is there.

From: Vicki (USA):

Is it possible to be in the wilderness and still be actively involved in a church? I identify with those who are in the wilderness and have left the church, and have considered doing the same, but I am getting mixed messages and until I am clear on my marching orders, I dare not move, yet I am so done with church programs. I think I'm an "In Church, Out of Church Christian", done with programs and empty worship, hungering for real ralationships centered on what God is doing, and longing to bear fruit even if it means pruning some very old branches.

From: Alistair (Australia):

We are still going to church but despair of it. I have wondered for some time whether the present Structure will be destroyed and the true bride will arise as a phoenix from the ashes, or whether the true church will be raised up beside the present one which will become even more irrelevant.

My wife & I have two aching desires deep within us. To see the arts redeemed, and to see the church actually being Jesus to the world around it.

Many of these people told me that they feel as though they simply "don't fit" with what is happening in their local churches. They hang around but they simply cannot get into what is happening:

From: Jill (New Zealand):

My husband and I, after being actively involved in Spirit-filled church life since 1965, have spent two years "out of church" and just recently started back again... in another fellowship.

However I sit there every Sunday feeling so out of place, and wondering what is wrong with me. I even have difficulty getting involved in corporate worship... yet at home... alone I feel so much closer to the Lord. We are not church hoppers, and have been very involved with home groups and Bible studies during our time in church. But since we have been "out there" I have found it far easier to communicate with others who are out of church for various reasons... some who have simply fallen thru' the cracks. We have no desire to be Lone Rangers doing our own thing, but it does seem to us, to be something God is doing.

From: Claudia (USA):

My husband and I were just having a discussion about whether or not we are being called out of the organized church. We are still attending a church on Sundays but, we do not seem to fit anywhere. We sit among thousands and hear a "good message" but "we are not connected to the body". We want to be. We have tried to connect only to be pushed out . We are seeing so much control in the local churches we attend. I know that being isolated is not the answer.

A number of these "In-church" people say they have noticed many others around them who seem restless and dissatisfied right now. This seems to be a very widespread phenomenon:

From: Peter & Doreen (New Zealand):

I have a tenuous tie with the Anglican church and have met so many people who are hungry for they-know-not-what! A restlessness is in their hearts, and like you say, 'They wander from church to church'....

From: Erlene (USA):

I have friends who have (for the most part) left the church. I am still going to mine. The reason is that I have NOT heard God tell me to do otherwise. I teach adult Bible study Sunday morning, some other Bible studies with various other people in their homes, and I know God has called me to teach. However, I am very unfulfilled with "church as usual". Frustrated that we do not see a lot more "signs following those who believe", and the routine of sameness. The gifts of the Spirit are very scarce, salvations are not happening on any grand scale, and church has become more of a Christian social club in my opinion....

From: Eileen (USA):

We are part of those Christians who have been totally unsettled at church. The only thing that is keeping us tied to this one church recently, is that our children are involved in the youth group and we feel they need that contact.

Every church we have been in, whether Pentecostal, Charismatic, Baptist... whatever... there is something missing in every church. I feel like the church of this generation is lacking the "fullness" of Christ. There always seems to be a major weak area. I'm not saying we are perfect Christians and know everything... that is far from true... but there is so much missing. I have learned and grown so much more (exceedingly) at home in my prayer closet seeking the Lord and studying His Word. My husband's and my spiritual growth has not come from attending church. It has come from spending time with HIM at home. Church has become more of a social hour than of truly seeking God. We should be doing the things that Jesus did (miracles, healing, deliverance, restoration, etc.) and even greater!! Especially in these last days!!

Many who wrote told me what an "empty" experience church has become for them, and how they have been wondering what on earth could be done to make things different:

From: Ruthie (USA):

I just seem to warm a seat in my church. The "activities" and the "programs" in the church are so empty. We have become a social club with a "bless me" mentality.... I find myself more eager to spend time alone with Jesus and feel His presence than I do seeking Him in a body of people that spend the entire service looking at their watches, trying to decide how much of their day off is going to be used up in the church service....

From: Hollie (USA):

I myself feel that I have been in a place of spiritual limbo for the past 4 or 5 years. The church I attend has some awesome services, programs are bursting out of the walls, etc, but it mostly just leaves me feeling unimpressed and listless in my heart. Because....

Because, maybe, I look at others, perhaps, and don't keep my eyes focused on Jesus (????)

Because I look at others, and after a great service, they are right back to doing all they were doing that wasn't quite perfect before the Lord. What good is a tremendous "touch" (goose bumps) from the Lord, if there is no lasting change when the goose bumps disappear??

I'm reluctant to witness to others in case they want to come to church with me. I feel that for the most part, bringing them to church, would/will only lead them into bondage to a church, and not into relationship with the Lord... I don't want someone to just "come to church" with me, I want them to "come to Jesus!"

Personal relationship of the individual with the Lord doesn't seem to be too stressed. It is mostly relationship with the pastor

*or the ministers, or our own ministry within the congregation.
I have no desire whatsoever for a ministry or leadership role
within the congregation. I've seen it all before, done much of it
myself, and am just really weary of it and unimpressed (as well
as unmoved) by it.*

*There is no greater joy, I think, than just going to visit the shut-
ins, the widows, the sick, the hurting, those who slip quietly out
the doors of the congregation, and no one notices because they
are so busy "ministering" to the lost. (The lost get loster, and
the saved get overlooked). Or, if they do notice someone hasn't
been coming for a while, they are too busy to really find out why
and/or where that person is. (Often, that very "busyness" is even
church-related!)*

*Yet at the same time, I am hungry. So desperately hungry to find
within a local congregation whatever it is within my spirit/soul
that is making me so terribly hungry and feeling dissatisfied
with what is being served to me within the local congregation.
I have examined my heart to see if it is "me". If there are things
I need to repent of, get taken care of, put under the blood, etc.
Of course there are. But, it isn't this alone, I think, that is
making me feel so starved spiritually.*

*I don't want a "good" service at my local church. I don't want to
participate in "more" programs and outreach ministries. I don't
want a position within the local congregation.*

*Maybe I just want to be fed. But, fed what? And why do I even
feel so starved spiritually? The Word says to "taste and see that
the Lord is good." Perhaps I am not "tasting". If so, I want to!
But I don't want to just taste something the pastor cooks up to
dish out each service. I don't want to be at a spiritual
smorgasbord and pick and choose what might satisfy me
spiritually, or give me Holy Ghost "goose bumps," that someone
else has prepared for me.
I just want GOD!!!*

From: Marilyn (USA):

It has been a long time since I have gotten anything out of church. The worship is weak... everything in a rush since we have services back to back. There is no time to let Holy Spirit in. But I want to tell you why I stay. I stay for the children. I am not there to get but to give. We can make the services for the children alive and meaningful. The children need us to be there. I get more out of giving to the kids then I do attending services.

From: Donna (USA):

I cannot tell you how many times I have gone to church desperate to meet with God only to leave disappointed and sometimes even in tears.

The churches that I have experienced here in America (in Oregon where I live, and in Texas) are so dead and dry (yes, the so called "Spirit-filled" ones) that I have to force myself to go, or can't force myself to go.

I wondered if there was something wrong with me for hating it so much, when all of my friends always gushed about "the presence of the Lord was so strong" or "that was really powerful." While my thought (never spoken of course) was UGH! I like my dentist better.

I love Jesus soooooooooo much and have such a good time just "hanging out" with Him at home, that I couldn't understand why I often felt so "icky" at church. I talk to so many of my unsaved friends and family, who without exception have been abused or even out and out stolen from by "Christians" and "ministers", and am constantly trying to convince them that that wasn't God that did that to them.

Unfortunately, most "Christians" give God such a bad name that the unsaved don't want anything to do with Him. I now pray constantly, "Lord, if I am misrepresenting you, stop me by any means necessary." I don't want to have to give an account on judgement day for all of the people that I kept away from God. Now that I know there are probably millions of us that feel the same way about "organized religion", I'll bet my socks that the exodus from the "church" is a move of God. He does say "Come out of her my people, and don't partake of her sins anymore."

Many of these "In-church" people told me that they are in a state of perplexity as to what to do or where to go. There seem to be so few options. They really do not see God moving in their church, but it does not seem much better elsewhere. What on earth can be done to remedy this malaise that has overtaken Western Christianity?

From: Sondra (Australia):

Although I have remained within the church system (uncomfortably) I just don't know what to do. I have been thinking it's all "me becoming strange and out of order."

I don't want to be out of the Body, just out of the "commercialised" church.... such a lack of intercession, seeking God, and quiet times of deep prayer. (In fact, none at all!!) And to be quite honest, no repentance at all! In fact, repentance seems a dirty word in our church. Far too uncomfortable to give it the amount of mileage it deserves and God requires for a healthy spiritual life. In fact, repentance has been pushed out in place of self-building and pride in all we do! Our church seems to promote itself as if it were so worthy of being right at the front of God's plans, purposes and blessings. I cringe inside my spirit, and feel sickened every Sunday when I have to sit through two hours of "Let's seek God" when all we seem to do is seek ourselves and have a good social time.

From: Cheryl (USA):

We have yet to 'let go' of church altogether but really, really want to, as we are frustrated and fed up with playing church.

We have been dedicated youth leaders for over 10 years and have been labelled as rebellious for our concerns on the state of the church the last few years. We find we have backed off from church but are hesitant to let go completely. Our feelings are this – if all of 'us' leave, who will tell the others who are feeling the same way that they are not alone and are not "weird"?

We are very dedicated in all aspects of our lives to God, and really are much closer to Him now than we have ever been. Funny how that works! We know many, many people who are either on the verge of leaving the church completely or have already done so. It is happening at an alarming rate here in Ontario. For so many of us to be feeling this way and making the same move, without prior knowledge of others going through the same territory, I cannot help but think that God is indeed leading this army out for a time, how long – who knows?

From: Tait (USA):

Since the first of the year I've been feeling so frustrated at my church and their worldly ways of doing things and their fearing man (the people in the pews) more than fearing the Lord that I've been feeling that I had to leave (because I was more focused on what was wrong than I was focused on the Lord). The Lord is very obviously moving at my church creating a new wineskin, but my frustration at people wanting to hold on to the old wineskin and rejecting even the possibility of the new is almost overwhelming.

From: Lea (USA):

Sometimes I feel like it would be easier for me to attend church regularly so I could avoid the concerned remarks from my Christian friends who believe that I am in disobedience. In fact, I have gone to church on occasion out of guilt but each time that I do, I feel like God reminds me again that He has called me out. Not out of fellowship with brothers and sisters, but out of the organized church.

On the occasion that I go, I feel so empty. I hear a pastor tell me how important it is to be part of a church. I have heard this message so much that it makes me wonder why so many pastors constantly remind us of this. I wonder whether they do not feel that God is big enough to meet us in our own homes without the organized worship, sermons and Sunday school for kids.

CHAPTER TEN

IS "REVIVAL" THE ANSWER?

A "Revival" in the Christian sense is defined as a powerful move of God to bring true 'restoration' and renewal – to return the church to something like its original 'Book of Acts' state – at least for awhile. There have been a number of powerful Reformations and Revivals down through history – some of which utterly transformed the church forever.

With the realization that thousands of people are leaving today's churches, many leaders want some kind of "answer" that will bring them back again. "What can we do to bring them back?" they ask. But they do not realize that many of these Out-of-church people are not interested in returning to "church as we know it". They are waiting for a new move – an entirely new 'Church' – something transformed by the power of God. In fact, it is clear that they want something far closer to the original church of the Bible. What they are talking about is large-scale Reformation and Revival. Something that will take us back to the full vitality, the faith and the power of the early Christians.

Now, one interesting thing about the original church in Jerusalem is that it was essentially an "outdoor" church. "Excuse me?" you say. "An outdoor church? I thought they met every day in the temple. That does not sound like an outdoor church to me."

Though few Christians today are made aware of this, it is absolutely beyond question that the Jerusalem church was based mainly out-of-doors and also in houses. Church buildings and Cathedrals were not invented for centuries.

The Book of Acts records that the Jerusalem believers met every day in a place called Solomon's Porch, which was in a giant open-air courtyard attached to the main Temple. This courtyard was known as "The Court of the Gentiles", and it was a huge, open, paved area – about the size of five-and-a-half football fields. Along one side ran the narrow covered area where the apostles would stand and preach – known as Solomon's Porch.

We know that the Jerusalem church numbered in the thousands right from the beginning, so if they wanted to gather together "as one" then the only place to do so was in a huge open area. Also, this was the most busy and crowded 'square' in the whole city. So if they wanted to get their message in front of the largest-possible audience, then this was the place to do it.

Now what does all this have to do with our discussion of the "Out-of-church" Christians? Well, it turns out that what they are wanting is really not so different from a lot of "In-church" Christians who call for a return to 'New Testament Christianity'. They are not so far apart after all. In fact, in many ways they are seeking exactly the same thing: A return to the original purity and power of the early church (which is what true 'Revival' is all about). Could it be that such a move of God may be the "meeting point" where a lot of In-church and Out-of-church people find common ground? Could this be the answer?

What is clear is that God wants His "original" church back. All the miracles, the unity, the piercing 'repentance' preaching, and everything else that made the early church what she was – this is clearly what He wants to restore. Because so much has been lost over the centuries. Our comparative impact today is minimal. And our petty divisions and denominations are killing us.

I think a lot of Christians would be surprised to learn how totally different the original was from that which we call "church" today. For one thing, in those days they had a completely UNITED church. (And I am not talking about 'ecumenism' here!) The simple truth is there were no 'denominations' at all. In fact, they would have been shocked even to hear of such a thing! This was "one" church – with no divisions, and no little groups separating themselves off and calling themselves by different 'labels'. After all, Jesus Himself had prayed, "That they all may be ONE... that the world may BELIEVE." Why is it that the world does not "believe" us today? Perhaps it is because we are not "one".

A lot of people lately have been emphasizing the fact that the early church met in houses (which is certainly true). But they seem to forget that the Jerusalem believers also gathered together in HUGE OPEN-AIR GATHERINGS. And this happened almost EVERY DAY – coming together "as one". All the believers from the entire city could gather together in this way.

Thus we can see that they had TWO different kinds of meetings in the Jerusalem church. One was the more intimate 'house-church' type meeting, where the believers from a local neighborhood would all gather together in someone's house – taking communion and flowing together in spiritual gifts – building each other up in unity and love. That was one kind of meeting. But the other kind was the huge outdoor type that we have been discussing. (A massive city-wide gathering where the apostles would preach and heal the sick, etc). These too happened all the time.

What the apostles were really doing here was continuing the ministry of Jesus – just as they had been commanded. Both Jesus and John-the-Baptist had a ministry that was largely in the open-air – out where the "common people" were. This was very important. They were called to reach the lost, not to hide themselves away behind four walls.

We in the church are doing the whole world a great disservice today. They almost never see us gathered together "as one", do they? In fact they hardly ever see us at all. We lock ourselves away in our separate little groups – behind four walls – out of sight and out of mind. No wonder we have so little impact on the world around us anymore. We are absenting ourselves from their lives.

But all of that is about to change. God has been speaking right around the globe in recent years about a coming "Great

Reformation" of the church – a great "shaking" that will return her to the way she was always meant to be.

It is interesting to note that many of the church's greatest Revivals and Awakenings down the centuries have involved a return to huge open-air gatherings. The Great Awakening of the 1740's (under Wesley, Whitefield and Tennant) was a prime example of this. It became commonplace for tens of thousands of people to gather in the open air. Likewise the 'Second Great Awakening' of the 1800's (beginning in Kentucky) which saw the origin of the 'camp-meeting', and had thousands gathering in open fields. Even the great 1859 Revival saw strong elements of this – especially in Ulster with her massive open-air prayer meetings.

I am convinced that God is about to move again in this way. He wants to restore the 'original' thing. He wants a church that gathers in "one accord" – right out where the people are. He wants "one" church – not many – a church that is pure and holy – "without spot or wrinkle or any such thing". And He wants a church that goes forth "destroying the works of the devil", just like Jesus did.

If God has to bring great "shaking" to see this kind of Christianity again, then that is what He will bring; whatever it takes. We are entering an era of great "change" in the church. In fact, I believe we are almost at the point of 'change or perish' in Western Christianity today. For God cannot live with a lukewarm church.

So where do the "Out-of-church" Christians fit into all this? Well, a large number of them believe that what they are going through right now is 'preparation' for this coming move of God. It really is significant how many of them wrote to me about this. They believe that in order to be fully prepared for what God is about to do, they need to 'unlearn' many of their old ways of "doing church" and prepare for the fact that God is about to do a whole new thing.

Here is a sampling of what they wrote on this subject:

From: Rowayne (South Africa):

I believe that God is busy with something totally different that will shake religion and tradition off the books. The time is coming that we will see a huge shift in the way church has been orchestrated. I believe church is going to the streets. Worship will absolutely combust onto the streetcorners and plains. Prayer will ascend from shopping malls and business venues. You will not have to go to church because church will be waiting for you outside!

The awesome transformation of a weak, powerless organisation into a potent Warrior Bride... Some of us have seen this wonderful shift in the heart of God many times and we are waiting and watching and it's not going to be much longer. Praise God!

From: Lea (USA):

I feel that the traditional way of "doing church" has had its era. I think that God is seeking out people who are willing to admit that we are starving and are not getting fed in the church today even though I hear pastors tell me that we are. I truly believe that we cannot be ready for the next move of God until we acknowledge that we are hungry and that the current structure is not working. I am waiting to see what God does and I think it will be outside of walls and especially outside of special programs and traditional Sunday morning agendas. And I look forward to the time when we as believers can unite under one umbrella and be privileged to be part of the next move that God is doing.

I don't think that everyone is called to leave the church but I do believe that some are and I am encouraged to hear that these people are responding. I'm excited to see what God is going to do with these people!

From: Sue (Australia):

In 1995 the Lord showed me that he was going to "shake the hell out of the church." Literally. He showed me that within the local church system there are demonic strongmen over some churches and they have the legal right to be there. He gave me Scriptures that "everything that can be shaken will be shaken." Any structure that is not established by the Lord will crumble and fall, eg. institutions, churches, colleges – anything that was not founded on the Rock Christ Jesus. The established system as we knew it was going to crumble. What had happened was that man had gotten in the way of God and his plan for his Kingdom. I am one of those waiting. I know that God will again use the men and women he has trained up and are outside the system. That what God has birthed into their lives will not be in vain. I felt I was hidden in the Cave of Adullam for 5 years. Last year at a prophetic conference I attended, I discovered others felt the same way.... Jesus is coming back for a glorious church.

From: Steven (Location unknown):

We have been outside for over three years, waiting for God to show us what to do next. This week I recieved a letter asking me to come teach pastoral leadership to a Bible School in the South Pacific. But what would I teach? My concept is totally changed from the "NORMAL" pastoral view. Is the Church ever going to be ready for the rooting out, tearing down, of the normal powerless system that causes the people to depend upon the church and the leaders instead of on God and Him ALONE?

From: Jim (Location unknown):

I jokingly call this an "Out of the Body experience" referring to the body of Christ. What it may turn out to be is an awakening that reveals the Church without walls.

From: Cathy (USA):

We have recently moved... there are 3 prominent Spirit-filled churches with the same doctrine for the most part. Yet, these three churches never mention the other or come together in unity for the area. They are all growing, as far as we can tell, and they all have nice buildings and programs to draw in as many people as possible... I can't help but wonder if, like in Transformations of Columbia, the leadership would come together... I heard one of the pastors from Columbia say: "The people were ready for unity, but the pastors were holding them back." It may not be the whole answer, but in my spirit I believe it could be a key step.

From: L.S. (USA):

I feel like I've been waiting a long time.... but I believe He is saying the Reformation is coming soon, and I will find a place in the new move of God.

From: Carroll (USA):

We have heard and continue to hear prophecies about the change that is coming in the church. Only we are hearing in part. Most of them do not realize that God is not moving us from one type of brick and mortar church to another, but to something outside the walls of the church as well.

We are not against church – but God wants to make some changes and we want to be with Him when He makes them.

Many people like ourselves who are unchurched are not alone – we are not lone rangers. The friends we have are not wandering around without direction. We are a part of the "Body" and the next big move of God will come in the marketplace and homes and it may well be that the ones "who miss out" could be inside the brick and mortar system. Because they are taught that everything must come from the system. They will have a hard time with the new move of God.

From: Mark (USA):

I feel in my heart that this mass of hungry and Christ-following people is God's own way of setting the stage for a huge reformational change.

As you can see, this sense of a coming Reformation or Revival is very prevalent amongst a lot of Out-of-church people. They see themselves as being in the 'wilderness' and headed for a Promised Land of Revival – a "new wineskin" for the church. But as I said earlier in this book, just like the children of Israel, the test will come when it is time to finally exit this wilderness.

I am convinced that many Out-of-church people certainly are "leadership" material, and it would not surprise me at all if God was preparing them for a leadership role in this coming move. But there is one thing they need to come to grips with: All of the greatest Revivals had strong leaders. This was totally crucial to their success. But can these Out-of-church people truly cope with this concept? I cannot help feeling that some (maybe many) could fall victim to the anti-leader, anti-authority, anti-Body attitudes that they have imbibed in the 'Out-of-church' scene (just like I did). A lot of them really don't believe in "LEADERSHIP" any more.

And if you do not believe in any but the mildest form of authority then it is very difficult to truly LEAD yourself. You may 'manage', but actual LEADING is a different matter. And without leaders who will use their authority to keep the devil out, any Revival will be infiltrated by the enemy in no time flat. I have seen this again and again as I have studied past Revivals. This is the main reason why the great Welsh Revival of 1904 finished after JUST ONE YEAR. We have an enemy who prowls around like a roaring lion and he hates Revivals. He has infiltrated and ruined many moves of God down through history, and if we give him the chance he will do it again. He loves to move into situations where there is a 'vacuum' of authority and no-one guarding the gates. I tell you, there is no such thing as a "leaderless" Revival. Or if there is, it does not last for long! Revivals must be guarded by leaders who are appointed to that place by God, and who are not afraid to stand up and be counted when the time comes. Such were Wesley, Booth, Finney and the like: strong leaders – all of them. And such were the apostles also; true 'fathers'. Revival and strong leadership go hand in hand.

The book of Acts is full of leaders who ACTED LIKE LEADERS. They were servants – yes. But they were also REAL LEADERS. Without them there would have been no Book of Acts. I wonder how long it will be before some Out-of-church people come to grips with this simple fact. (It took me a very long time).

So I have to ask these questions: Are today's Out-of-church people truly ready to help LEAD a new move of God? Or are many of them actually afraid to "lead"? Are they ready to assume responsibility and authority where required? Or do they believe in a kind of "leaderless" Revival? Are they ready to become "joiners" in the true sense of the word? Or is suspicion and 'standoffishness' now a large part of their make-up? Are they actually ready to be knit into a Body? Or will they eventually find some excuse to remain distant and detached? These are all crucial questions. And they are the very things that will be tested when the time comes. Have these people truly RENOUNCED all the things that they need to renounce?

REPENTANCE TO SWEEP THE CHURCH

It is obvious that even though there are many issues of "structure" that need to be dealt with today, the REAL issues (the ones that really matter) are issues of the HEART. The church is sick and ailing because her heart is sick and ailing. It is not so much a matter of the "boxes" that she lives in or the style of meetings that she has. These are secondary factors. It is the HEARTS of God's people that really need work. And that is what any true Revival must do first – cleanse and purify the hearts of His people. Fixing the 'structural' things can come later. The heart is what really matters. And thus a great wave of REPENTANCE must come first (just like every true Revival down through history).

I know a number of people in the house-church movement who believe that if we can just get the right house-based structure, then everything else will follow. Some spend hours discussing 'plurality of elders' and house-church formats, etc. They seem to believe that if they can change the "boxes", then everything else will come right. I am sorry, but I have to disagree. A change of HEART is what is needed – primarily and above all. And it is Revival that will bring this about. Remember, in the early church it was the OUTPOURING at Pentecost that came first – and then the new structures were built around that. Revival must first come and transform the hearts of God's people before anything else. To try and form a 'new wineskin' without the new wine is simply putting the cart before the horse.

Like many people, I am convinced that a great Revival is coming – a flood of God's Spirit that will bring the church to her knees in deep repentance and transformation. And through this there will come a 'new wineskin' and an enormous harvest – with many new leaders raised up by God.

So will many of today's Out-of-church people be amongst this new leadership? I have no doubt that they will. God did not put them through all this training for nothing. But timing is the key. Sometimes it takes a "crisis" for new leadership to be allowed to arise. "Cometh the hour, cometh the man" as the saying goes. And it is never more true than in times of Reformation or Revival. Suddenly the new leaders arrive, as if from nowhere – prepared for years in the secret place by God. So it has always been with the greatest Revivals. Timing is all.

As we have seen in this chapter – in fact this whole book – there are a group of Christians in the world today who have left the comfort of routines and friends and familiar surroundings, to set off towards something new, not knowing exactly where they are going or how they will get there. Just knowing that they had to go. They heard a call, they tasted a vision, and off they went. It was a brave thing to do and a lot of them have my deepest admiration. If they can make it through the desert, nothing is surer than that many of them will make wonderful leaders of God's people. But it is getting out of that 'wilderness' mindset that is the key thing. I personally believe that a great number of them will make it through. We are living in momentous days.

So is this huge Out-of-church movement a sign that something unprecedented lies just ahead? Is the massive groundswell of "dissatisfaction" amongst multitudes of Christians evidence that dramatic change is just around the corner? Certainly we would have to conclude that something major is going on. This thing is way too big to be mere coincidence. There is something very unusual taking place – on a worldwide scale that only God could orchestrate.

Are we about to see a new breed of leader come in from the desert – prepared for years for this time – ready to usher in a new move of God's Spirit? Is another great 'Street-Revival' approaching? Well, one thing is certain: We desperately need one. Only time will tell. But the signs are there that something of this order of magnitude is definitely building. It seems beyond question that God is on the move in a new way in this generation. And He is doing something quite radical. Or perhaps it is something so old that it just seems radical – because we have never seen its like before.

VISIT OUR WEBSITE-

www.revivalschool.com

CPSIA information can be obtained at www.ICGtesting.com
Printed in the USA
LVOW122331180812

294730LV00005B/14/P